What Other

"This book has been instrumental in my life because it has opened my eyes to the freedom of forgiveness. It has encouraged me that I am not alone in my journey. It has renewed my sense of hope."

~Jamie

"I finally feel like I am not alone, and my situation is not unique to only me. I need every pearl."

~Regina

"This book helped me to set my sights on what God wants to refine in ME to better my marriage and my family! It gave the deeper perspective of the roll I play in my marriage, and the responsibility I need to take in surrendering to Him on the daily."

~Jasmine

NANA'S PEARLS

Finding Hope in Your Blended Family Marriage

MEGAN BOTTOM

This is a work of fiction. All of the characters, organizations, and events portrayed in this novel are either products of the author's imagination or are used fictitiously.

Nana's Pearls © 2020 by Megan Bottom. All rights reserved.

Published by Author Academy Elite
PO Box 43, Powell, OH 43065
www.AuthorAcademyElite.com

Identifiers:
LCCN: 2020916538
ISBN: 978-1-64746-471-4 (paperback)
ISBN: 978-1-64746-472-1 (hardback)
ISBN: 978-1-64746-473-8 (ebook)

Available in paperback, hardback, and e-book

All Scripture quotations, unless otherwise indicated, are taken from the Holy Bible, New International Version®, NIV®. Copyright © 1973, 1978, 1984 by Biblica, Inc.™ Used by permission of Zondervan. All rights reserved worldwide.

Dedication

Dwayne, thank you for being my rock, my disaster relief, my storm chaser, my best friend, my Spiritual leader, my lover . . . my husband. Love you!

Hannah, Tanna, Rachael, Trace, Jacob and Teiler (T.J.), seriously, literally, this book would not be possible without you. The struggles, the fights, the victories, the chaos, and the love is so worth it all. If I had a chance to do it again, knowing what I know now, I absolutely would 1000's of times over. I am so proud of each one of you. You guys are amazing. Love you!

My parents, while the lessons you taught me are vast, teaching me to have a family full of grace and forgiveness will always be enough. Love you!

My sister, the most driven person I know; if I could get just an ounce of your drive and half of your motivation, I would be forever grateful. Thank you for tolerating me. Love you!

Jamie, your words of encouragement, your patience, and your wisdom were invaluable gifts that I didn't know I needed in this journey. Love you!

Evie, what else can I say but THANK YOU! Love you!

Denise, thank you for having a no-spending limit friendship bank. Thank you for never giving up on me. Thank you for dropping those clothes off at the wrong house. Thank you for morning garage sales. Thank you for leading and guiding me toward my Savior. Thank you for being there (still) for my girls. Thank you for the late-night rescue phone calls. Thank you for the popcorn and diet cokes. Thank you for the taco soup, and the big soup pots. Thank you for being you! STRAWBERRIES! Love you!

Gina & Kim, obviously, you don't know each other, and it might be strange to lump you two together, but the kids I love and cherish, the children I adore and am so proud of would not be who they are today without you two. Thank you for all you have, and continue to do for them.

Author's Note

Who would've thought this would be the hardest to write? I am not an author. I am a wife, a mother and a stepmother that has navigated the same journey that I am assuming you're navigating right now. I am a lot of things, but an author. . . I am not. I feel I must explain some things before you delve into this story. What you're about to read is mainly fictional. One thing I learned while writing this is that my experience is unique, but it is not that spectacular. I want to take a moment to acknowledge the "real" part of the journey you are about to dive into.

Owen's character was created from my husband, Dwayne. There are funny quirks that I adore about the best gift (other than Jesus) that I have been given. My husband does clean when he's anxious, upset, or nervous. My husband had to learn, with me, a lot of these lessons, just as Owen did.

We have six kids total, and I realize that Owen and Teá only have four. No children were intentionally left out of this story, the kids were mainly fictional, and the interactions involving the children in the book are my creation as well. I did this intentionally to avoid hurting our kids if our journey was published for all to read.

There is one real story, though, and for that, I want to apologize officially to our oldest daughter. Hannah, I don't know if you remember that women's retreat, or if you understand the impact it had on me. I ask your forgiveness for any ugliness I displayed due to my unforgiving spirit. I am so far from perfect.

I do have a Nana. She was an incredible person, and my memories of her are expansive. Unfortunately, she was robbed of all of her memories due to a horrible condition called Alzheimer's. Nana did not give me gifts of pearls, like Teá's Nana did, BUT my Nana and Papa gave me a beautiful legacy. Their gift to me was a successful and loving marriage, blessed with three children, nine grandchildren, seventeen great-grandchildren, and three great-great-grandchildren. Thank you, Papa and Nana, your legacy will continue!

Elle's is an actual restaurant that I worked for, and I love the regulars there. The owners, Lynnferd and Sarah, will always hold a special place in my heart for seeing Dwayne and me through some of our struggles. The "regulars" as well, are very real. They have a bond that centered around their small town for generations, and I appreciate the wisdom they bestowed on me in the short time I was part of their story. The next round is on . . . well, not me! If you ever find yourself in Crete, Nebraska, look them up—Elle's on Main. You won't be disappointed. P.S. Sorry Lynnferd, for making it a Husker's bar.

Finally, Jenni is a great friend and mentor. The beginning of my marriage to Dwayne was hard, and if it weren't for her friendship, support, and guidance, there is no telling where we would be today.

••• | •••

Forgiveness

At the end of the day, a loving family should find everything forgivable.

~Jim Butcher

HARLEY SAT IN front of Teá in the white Suburban driven by the pastor's wife. Coming back from a women's retreat, Teá had thought it was a great idea to invite Harley to the event; they could use the alone time to bond with each other. At twelve, and being the oldest of the kids, Harley was responsible beyond her years. Teá would rather have brought one of her own girls, Mia or Ava, but they were with their dad the weekend of the retreat. Honestly, they probably were not old or mature enough to attend. Teá thought Harley was a great addition to the women who went, because Harley seemed to have a better understanding of faith and had developed a closer relationship with God. Teá had been excited about the retreat and she had looked forward to it for weeks.

Harley was sound asleep while they drove, and Teá could make out the way her eyelashes would twitch as the lights from the passing cars shone on her eyes. It instantly reminded Teá of Owen's eyes—he always had wild dreams that caused his eyes to flutter and twitch all night long. She loved Owen with the kind of love that made her want to memorize the way he looked when he slept.

• • •

Teá had nothing but time, so her mind wandered back to the beginning of her relationship with Owen. She remembered that she was the one who originally agreed to talk to him, after he pursued her for a bit, but could not quite remember what had drawn her to him. She did remember, the love came hard and fast. Once they began their relationship, things moved quickly. Whatever it was that initially brought them together, was going to have to be enough to keep this marriage going, if it was going to succeed. That would have to be the thing that provided them the will to overcome the issues they had with their children. *Maybe it would just be easier to walk away*, Teá couldn't help but wonder. Owen always said there was no way they were going to divorce, that this was the divorce-proof marriage. She had also been talking to Nana recently, and Nana kept telling her, "There is always hope." Teá would keep her response to herself because she wasn't prepared for the lecture that was sure to follow, but the truth was, Teá hated hope.

Was there hope for her and Owen? Was there hope that one day Teá and Owen would be a real family? Would they ever have a divorce-proof marriage? Teá found herself lost in the memories of when they first met, when they were getting to know each other, and became familiar with the idea of a relationship. The newness of their love was refreshing and fun. They stayed up all night talking on the phone, in endless hours of conversation about nothing and everything all at the same time. Teá remembered the nights, but she also remembered the exhausted mornings. Her and Owen would drudge through their days like zombies, but so filled with excitement that they couldn't stop smiling. They looked forward to the next time they got to see each other, talk to each other or embrace one another.

It was easy to fall in love with Owen, but Teá couldn't help wondering if the days of their courtship were the best part of their relationship. It was harder now—the hours of delightful conversation had turned into tense arguments about raising the children each of them brought to their marriage. The flirtatious giggles and romantic innuendos had been forgotten, replaced by a routine and tedious life.

Their meeting was so untraditional. They met through mutual friends at a BBQ, but they lived several miles apart. Due to the distance, as well as the children they both had, dates were few and far between, and the majority of their conversations happened through texts and phone conversations. They really didn't *court* each other, but their communication skills were strong and developed by the time they actually said their vows. The vows that solidified their commitment, the vows that they whispered so intimately before their pastor and his wife. They entered their marriage with so much... hope. The thousands of text messages and hours of phone calls taught them how to talk to each other, listen, and communicate love to each other, without being physically present. Teá constantly doubted whether or not this time, this hope, was going to be different. Owen started the tradition of praying with each other early on in their relationship. Each night they both snuck away for a few minutes and quietly prayed through the phone with and for one another. She remembered so vividly the feelings that those prayers elicited: excitement, love, devotion, and a feeling of...hope.

• • •

Now, in the car ride after the conference, Teá was reminded of the idea of hope. She asked herself, *what is hope anyway? Is it a feeling? Could it be a wish? Does it describe an emotion?* She didn't know, but what she did know was that it was always hopeless, always disappointing, and this time the situation was no different. Was there hope for her and Owen? Or was this relationship doomed to fail too? He always seemed so optimistic, so trusting, and sure. Teá didn't know, although she couldn't help but let the curiosity take over and wonder what a future without him or his kids in her life would look like. She couldn't quite make out the fuzzy areas. She couldn't determine if a life without Owen was either the best dream ever or the worst nightmare imaginable. The future without Owen, and without Harley and Lincoln, could be a glorious reprieve from the stress they were all under. It could also be another thing that didn't work out—another thing that failed. She'd have to start over...again...with nothing.

Failure was familiar. It seemed inevitable, almost comfortable. Could she handle another divorce? What would her own kids, Ava and Mia, think? Would they be able to adjust again to life without Owen and his kids? The fuzzy parts of the failure were what kept her where she was. Teá knew the transition to life without Owen would be difficult and she didn't want to remember the loneliness she had before he came into her life. Teá loved Owen, and honestly, deep down, she loved Harley and Lincoln too.

Teá yawned and drew her attention to the back of Harley's head. It was late, and she wondered why she had agreed to come to the stupid conference. Why had she invited Harley in the first place? She was angry with Owen because he hadn't taught Harley appropriate manners. Why did she have to be so embarrassed over things Harley did? She had never been so disgusted in her entire life—thoughts of anger, frustration, and confusion about it kept repeating in her head. If Teá were honest, she would have admitted that the anger was dramatic, but she was frustrated with having the same fights, the same conversations, and the same embarrassment she felt when their kids—Owen's kids—didn't behave.

The retreat had been awesome, as anticipated, but all of the convictions, lessons, and wisdom gained had been fast forgotten. Teá's anger wouldn't allow any of the lessons to stay rooted with her for long. After the conference, the group of ladies they were traveling with decided to try Chic-fil-A for dinner. The restaurant was closing, but the employees were gracious enough to let all nine ladies in the group stay and eat. It was too rushed. Not only was the restaurant wanting to close, but the group still had a three-hour car ride back home. Everybody was packing up, grabbing their purses, and throwing away their trash while the employees of the restaurant mopped around the ladies as they were hastily making their way to the door.

That was when Harley said she had to use the restroom. Teá could feel her pulse quicken at the announcement, and she looked at Harley in a way that could only communicate, *you had better hurry!* Harley shrugged off the look, almost as if she hadn't even noticed the icy glare from Teá and sauntered off to the bathroom.

The ladies piled back into the seats of the SUV for the long, late drive home. The excitement from the retreat was still palpable; everybody had ideas, convictions, and fresh revelations to share with each other. They couldn't help but talk about the speaker's instructions and wisdom. The worship and prayer time at the end obviously had a big, emotional impact on everybody. They were still excited, and sleep wasn't yet possible; it was late, and it had been a very long day. The clock was ticking. There was no sign of Harley from the restaurant, and the more impatient sighs that Teá heard from the other ladies, the more she could feel the anger welling up.

This had been a trick of Harley's since Teá married her dad. Whenever she wanted attention, she made everybody wait for her. She would suddenly have to use the restroom, or she would have to make sure her shoes were *just right*. Her hair had to be brushed one more time, or she had some other lame excuse Harley concocted to make everybody wait for her. While Harley's antics seemed innocent enough, and Owen dismissed them as her little quirks, Teá had no patience for it. At twelve, Harley should have more respect and less control than that in the home. Now, though, to play these games with the women from the church, was pushing Teá's nerves past the breaking point.

Teá hardly knew these women and she desperately wanted to impress them. She had struggled to fit into Owen's church family since their marriage. Teá didn't have much in common with many of the women. After the divorce and re-marriage, it seemed Teá struggled to fit in anywhere. She wasn't a full-time mom to anybody. With the 50/50 custody arrangement she had with her girls' father, and everybody knowing that Owen's kids were not actually *hers*, she questioned herself, whether or not she was even a mom at all. So, while she was still a newlywed with Owen, she already had kids—not fitting the newlywed ideal. While she had kids in certain age groups, like all moms, none of her kids fell into the same situation or schedule as anyone else at the church—not fitting into the typical mom norm either. She wasn't a newlywed, a traditional mom, or an empty nester, so Teá always felt as though she really didn't belong. The retreat with the women from her church was her opportunity to make some new friends and to share her life, frustrations, dreams, and desires with other people. Of course, that would be the night when Harley pulled her stunt.

Twenty minutes ticked by, then thirty. Tea's fury was growing by the minute. She could not believe Harley was being this disrespectful. Finally, Teá marched back into the now-closed restaurant. She pounded loudly on the single-stall bathroom door, and Harley opened the door with a smile, drying her hands. "What? I had to use the bathroom," Harley exclaimed with a smile and skipped back to the waiting women, without so much as an apology for keeping them waiting. She climbed into her seat and fell fast asleep.

Teá whipped out her cell, and typed furiously to Owen, blinking back the hot tears that were steaming just behind her eyes.

"Harley just spent 30 minutes in the bathroom at the Chick-fil-A. We are on our way now."

● ● ●

"Is Harley okay? How was the retreat?"

● ● ●

"I don't care if Harley is okay or not. She pulls this stunt every time! I am so embarrassed. I can't even talk to these women anymore."

● ● ●

"Calm down. Did you ask if Harley was okay?"

● ● ●

"You cannot be serious. Are you really going to take her side again? Of course, she's okay. She just wanted all the attention on her. She wanted everybody waiting for her, like always. I have been telling you this for months. It's her way of taking control."

● ● ●

"I just texted Harley, I hope she's feeling all right."

● ● ●

"She is fine! She is sleeping soundly! Do you not trust me to take care of her? Why do you always take her side?"

● ● ●

"I guess if somebody spends 30 minutes in the bathroom, I worry that they're not feeling well. Didn't realize I was taking sides. How was the retreat?"

● ● ●

"You always take her side, and I don't understand. We have got to get this under control. Things cannot continue this way!"

● ● ●

Of course, Owen took Harley's side. Of course, Owen didn't even acknowledge how embarrassing it must've been for Teá around all the ladies from church. The *princess* was always in the right because she had him wrapped around her little finger.

Teá could hear the chatter of the excited women in the car, but she was so full of her own battles they were just background noise to the fight and anger raging inside her. She closed her eyes and tried to sleep to make the drive go faster, but the destination the car was headed—home to Owen—was not where she wanted to go either.

The next morning, Teá was up early, having hardly slept. Owen had obsessively cleaned until they got home, until well after midnight. Owen cleaned when there was tension; it was his way of taking control of a situation. Teá poured coffee into her cup from the sparkling pot in the immaculate kitchen and giggled lightly to herself about her husband's obsessive cleaning habits. She quietly padded to the living room to call Nana in her slippers and robe, knowing Nana would be awake, reading her Bible. Nana was always up early, wearing down the already worn pages of her sacred book.

Nana picked up on the second ring. "Good morning Teá, you're up early." It always surprised Teá—the advances in technology that Nana seemed to learn overnight.

She responded, "You learned how to read your caller ID?" Teá heard Nana chuckle.

"No, dear. It talks to me now in a robot voice. Surely you didn't call to see if I was awake or to make sure I knew how to use my phone. How was your retreat?"

"Oh, Nana, it was awful. Harley made all the women wait for like, 30 minutes in the Chick-fil-A on the ride home. She claimed she had to go to the bathroom, but she really just wants all the attention on her. It's so rude. She didn't apologize, and I'm just over it all!" Teá came up briefly for air, but her rant continued, "Owen doesn't care. He's content raising unappreciative brats that always get their way, and he always takes their side. I'm tired of being the evil step-mom.

I'm tired of being embarrassed for the kids' behavior. I'm tired of not having any control. I'm just so tired, Nana." The tears stayed tucked behind her eyes, but they were hot and ready to roll.

Nana could hear Teá's voice break and she answered with her typical, "Mmmhmmm." There was silence on the line for a minute, but Nana always took her time to respond. She asked calmly again, "How was the retreat?"

Teá laughed, annoyed. "Nana, I know you heard me."

Nana responded, "Of course I did, dear, but did you hear me? I wanted to know how the retreat was, not how Harley acted."

The tears began to fall; Teá couldn't hold them back any longer. "Nana, I don't care about the retreat. Don't you understand? Doesn't anybody ever understand?" She was mad now, furious. The anger she felt for the entire situation welled up, and she was ready to unleash it.

Nana answered as calmly as ever, "Of course I understand, but again, I don't think you do." The calmness in Nana's voice usually brought comfort to Teá, but in this situation, she got more and more angry. She heard Nana take a sip of her coffee, adjust the phone, take a deep breath, and exclaim, "This is a perfect example."

Teá interrupted her, "Nana, I really don't want one of your lectures or insights right now. I was just hoping to vent," exasperated by Nana's apparent lack of understanding.

"Well, venting and complaining isn't going to help anything."

Of course, she was right but Teá just could not handle a lecture this time. "Nana, I just ..."

"You just what, dear? You just want everybody to feel sorry for *you*? You just want all the attention on *you*? *You* just want to be right, justified in your anger?"

Teá interrupted her beloved grandma again, "I've got to go. I hear Owen coming down the hall. I'll call you later,

Nana. I love you." Teá lied to her Nana, and then hung up the phone. She sat there on the couch by herself and sobbed.

Nana was the only constant for Teá; she was the only one she knew who would be there no matter what. Teá's parents were great; they made sure that she and her sister wanted for nothing. Their love and devotion for each other was to be envied, and her family life growing up had been everything a kid could ask for. Teá was always fond of her Nana, her maternal grandmother. She was the person Teá didn't ever want to disappoint, but to whom she wasn't afraid to confess her wrong doings. Nana was quick with a hug but just as quick with a lesson. Her love for God was fierce, and Teá always admired that about her, although she couldn't ever find herself that committed to her own personal relationship with Jesus. She felt a little guilty for lying and hanging up on her Nana, but Nana hadn't given Teá what she was hoping to receive either.

Once she pulled herself together, she got up to take a shower and wake the kids for school. The morning routine was quiet. Harley and Lincoln seemed to feel the tension in the house and Ava and Mia were with their dad for the week. Owen left for work without a word to Teá. She dropped the kids off and headed back to the house she had moved into with Owen and the kids over a year ago, after the wedding. She still didn't feel like she was at home there. It was hard to fit into somebody else's domain. She always felt like she was a guest, always on the outside looking in. It also felt like her kids were merely sleeping over, as opposed to actually living in their room they shared with Harley.

As usual, Teá found herself wandering around the house with nothing to do. She had struggled to find work since moving to this new community. It wasn't far from her childhood home and was still close enough to keep the every-other-week schedule with Ava and Mia. If she had kept her job, though, there would be the drudge of a daily commute, on top of the added responsibility of Owen's kids full-time. If working was going to be an option for her, the job would have to be in the community in which they were now living.

Since the house was already spotless, thanks to Owen's way of relieving tension, she padded around the house aimlessly, until the familiar whistle tone that signaled a new text message pulled Teá out of her pity party.

• • •

"And hope does not put us to shame, because God's love has been poured out into our hearts through the Holy Spirit, who has been given to us." The preview from Nana's text flashed across her phone screen.

Astonished, Teá opened the text to respond. "Nana...who taught you how to text?"

• • •

"Thought I'd remind you that hope never disappoints."

• • •

"I hate hope, Nana, I told you that."

• • •

"You don't hate hope; you don't know hope." She chuckled to herself that her Nana was, first of all, texting, and secondly, telling her again that she didn't understand. Teá didn't understand a lot of things, the least of which was the idea of hope. She had nothing but time today. Her usual house-keeping routine was interrupted by the already-spotless house, and the lack of sleep the night before had made her less than motivated to find something to do. Teá again got lost her in thoughts.

No, she didn't understand hope! She didn't understand how the ex-husband that she had thought would be hers for eternity could have said things like, "I hope to find somebody else that can make me happy." How somebody could give well-wishes with a trite, "Hope everything works out for the best," or the empty, "Hope that doesn't happen to us," that Owen exclaimed when they talked about their previous failed marriages. *Hope does disappoint*, Teá thought, as she re-read Nana's text message. *Hope always disappoints.*

• • •

The week trudged on uneventfully for the family. Teá always felt out of place when she didn't have her girls to tend to and when it was just Owen, Harley, and Lincoln. When the kids were away at school, and Owen at work it gave Teá a lot of time to think. For whatever reason, whenever she was angry, her thoughts always returned to the same dark ugliness. She remembered her failed marriage to the girls' dad and the disastrous relationship that followed the divorce. She remembered the predicament she was in now, and continued to wallow in the belief that there was no hope. A friend from church asked her one time, on one of her dark days, if she had enough hope to hold on. Teá answered, "Yes," confidently, only because she was afraid of the alternative.

On these days, it was not uncommon for Teá to stay in her pajama's. There was no reason to get dressed to drop the kids at school, and once back home she found solace in her bed. She would play mindless games on her cell phone or doze off for hours on end, never feeling fully rested. Ashamed of not being the wife she had promised Owen, she would hurry to get dressed, hoping to at least look put together when the kids got home, and Owen got off work. The truth was, though, that the few hours between everybody coming home and bedtime could sometimes be painful, especially when she was angry, confused, and frustrated.

Teá wanted to be the wife to Owen she knew she was capable of being. She wanted to be the mom to Lincoln and Harley they deserved, and she wanted to be happy her girls had such a loving father that cared for them as well as he did. She wasn't, though. She wasn't happy about any of those things. She was disappointed in herself for what felt like another failed relationship, she was frustrated that Owen's kids were not who she thought they should be, and she was angry that she had to share her girls, her own flesh and blood, with somebody—even if he was a great father.

Teá often found herself in this funk for days and it would always happen after a fight with Owen or a disagreement about the kids with Todd, her ex-husband. She didn't understand why it was so hard to fight through the fog. Sometimes she quit trying, and she would wait for the sun to shine again. Occasionally Teá felt ill, got headaches, or lost her appetite. One time she even convinced Owen that she had the flu, but the truth was, it was an excuse to isolate herself from the hopelessness she felt with every failure.

A few days after the conference, a postal service envelope arrived in the mailbox addressed to Teá. It was marked with Nana's familiar scrawl. Inside was a meticulously wrapped little box. Teá unwrapped the box to find a single small black pearl. It was beautiful, ebony but with a mysterious cloudiness throughout. There was a delicate sheet of paper, hand-written, with the pearl, revealing one single word: *Forgiveness.*

Teá knew as soon as she saw the pearl, it was going to be another pearl of wisdom from Nana. She received them periodically in different times of her life. She received a gorgeous white pearl when she started showing an interest in boys— the pearl of wisdom accompanying it: *Purity.* She received many pearls when she first married her girls' dad, even a full string of them to wear with her gown. More pearls arrived with the birth of each child, but it had been a while since she had received one. The divorce didn't produce any pearls of wisdom from Nana. Nana's strength was everything Teá had needed at that time, although she really didn't believe Nana's wisdom could dispel the hurt she experienced. Courting and marrying Owen didn't produce any pearls of wisdom from Nana either. Teá assumed Nana had already given her all those pearls with the first marriage. There was nothing new to offer with this one except hope, which Teá didn't have much of.

Teá picked up the smooth, silky pearl and rolled it around in her fingers. She was pretty sure it was her only black pearl—all the rest were varied hues of milky white, some with a little yellow mixed in, pink, or baby blue, but never black. Teá knew there was significance to the dark pearl, but she was curious about Nana's thought process in picking this particular black pearl for the word *Forgiveness*. Teá made herself a cup of coffee, grabbed her new pearl and her phone, and settled in for a long talk with Nana.

"Hello, dear."

"Nana, who taught you how to text?"

"Oh, I'm loving it, but I just do not understand the abbreviations. Have people forgotten how to spell, too?"

Teá chuckled at her Nana's observation—maybe people were forgetting how to spell. She made a mental note to write out every word when texting Nana.

"I received your pearl today. Why is it black?"

Nana answered quickly, like she already knew the questions Teá would have. "I thought it fitting."

That didn't ease Teá's curiosity at all. "Fitting for what?" Teá caught herself sounding a little impatient.

"Oh, dear, did you not get the wisdom note?" Nana sounded concerned.

"Yes, Nana. Forgiveness. What does that have to do with the black pearl?"

"Because I'm afraid that's how your heart is starting to look." Nana sounded like she almost enjoyed the little insult. Teá did not have a black heart!

"Be nice, Nana."

"If you don't start working on some of the issues you are holding onto so tightly, my dear, you're going to be standing out just as that pearl does amongst the sea full of white pearls. You want to know one of my favorite things about our family?"

"Do I have a choice?" Teá joked with her Nana, but she was excited to hear the story Nana had to tell her.

"I love that we forgive," Nana said, sounding annoyed with her granddaughter's attitude.

"I forgive, Nana. I am a very forgiving person." Teá felt she had to defend herself against her Nana's unfair assessment.

"I agree. Most of the time you have no problem extending grace. In fact, it's one of the things I love about you, too. Sometimes, though, you can hold onto a grudge so tightly that you block the blessings right in front of you," Nana said confidently.

Usually, receiving the pearls were joyous occasions. Teá had such fond memories of the pearls in her jewelry box, but sometimes the pearls were not so fun to receive. She could tell this one was going to be a fight.

"Teá, listen. When you hung up on me the other morning, lying about Owen being awake, you were so angry you couldn't see straight. You weren't hearing a word I was saying, and you were probably a bear to be around at home. I'd even guess you probably still aren't being very pleasant to your family."

Teá started to protest but, already defeated, she let out a sigh of admission instead.

"You are so angry with everybody and everything, that the littlest thing sets you off into a fit of rage. You might not be physical with your emotion, but your attitude and words reflect how you feel more than you realize."

"Nana, it has been so hard." Teá could feel the familiar sting of the tears welling in her weary eyes.

"There is no doubt. It has been really hard, but have you considered how hard it has been on everybody around you, too? I'm not saying you don't have the right to be angry. That is not my judgment to make. What I am saying is that you have to forgive."

"Harley continues to play this game, though…"

Nana cut Teá off. "It's not about Harley. That's not what I'm talking about at all."

Teá was confused. She knew the pearl delivery came because of the conversation about the retreat. "If not Harley, who?"

"Todd."

Teá was even more confused, Nana was bringing up Tea's first marriage with this? The girls' father. The marriage had always been difficult. Todd and Teá had fought constantly the entire time they were married. Those fights were more like wars, where battle fields were strewn with words of anger and defeat, each of them seeing who could hurt the other most deeply. The more the fights happened, the more convinced Teá became that the marriage was over. Once the big *D* word was uttered, things ended peacefully, and they had an amicable relationship now. They still argued over issues with the girls, but they both had moved on. Todd was re-married before Owen and Teá were. What was Nana's concern with Todd?

"Owen," Nana continued before Teá could ask any clarifying questions.

Teá didn't have anything to forgive Owen for. Owen and Tea's love was fierce. It was the kind of love people looked their entire lives for. They fought, but they were devoted and true to their relationship. The fights, unlike fights with Todd, were respectful and useful. Owen was the man of Tea's dreams, her soul mate, her companion. While she still wondered if their relationship was going to withstand the struggles of raising their kids, she did not have to forgive Owen for anything.

"Melissa," Nana continued listing names, offering no other words or explanations. Teá was still trying to make sense of everything Nana had said about forgiveness and Nana threw this one like a left hook, out of nowhere. Harley and Lincoln's mom? Owen's ex-wife? That's too much after everything she had done. Melissa was a mess. She had left Owen with no excuse, no explanation. She simply left. Owen admitted some things he did to cause problems in their marriage, but Melissa just packed up and left after fifteen years of marriage and two beautiful children.

"Adam." It was another name that took Teá's breath away. How could Nana even bring this one up? They had an unspoken agreement, in which that name, that time, was never to be mentioned again.

Hot tears fell heavily with the mention of Adam, a boyfriend Teá had met right after the divorce from Todd. The relationship Teá and Adam had had was explosive and ugly, encompassing the very reason Teá hated hope. Adam would scream at Teá and throw things, the abuse at times happening in front of the girls. The entire ordeal lasted less than a year but it was enough to leave deep scars in Teá's life, not to mention heart. It took a while for the family to recover from the disaster that Adam left in his wake.

"Harley." Wasn't this where it all started . . .with Harley? Now Nana gets back to her? Teá's head was spinning from the mention of all these names. She was more confused than ever with all the emotion they stirred up inside her, feelings Teá was sure she'd buried.

Harley had taken the brunt of her mom's disappearance; she was so young and had been expected to be the mom of the house. She took on the responsibility for her little brother, and protected her dad and brother fiercely, which always made Teá feel like an outsider.

"Lincoln," Nana continued. Teá didn't have a chance to process. Nana just kept naming names.

Lincoln was such a cool kid. He was happy-go-lucky most of the time and didn't cause any kind of trouble. Teá had always wished for a boy, but Lincoln never fully devoted himself to her the way Teá had hoped he would. Teá never shared that disappointment with anybody, not even Nana. She knew Lincoln was loyal to his father, his sister, and strangely, Melissa, too . . . still.

"God." Nana said the last name, confidently.

"Stop. Wait. I don't have to forgive God. I trust Him. I know Him. I don't have to forgive Him." The mention of God was too much. Teá needed to think, to process, and to understand why these names still held such ugly emotions. She defended God as if on auto-pilot, like her brain knew what to say before her heart could catch up. But once Teá got started, it all spewed out. "What does Todd have to do with this? Why are you talking about Adam and Harley? You said it wasn't about Harley. What are you saying, Nana?" Teá's face was red and tear-stained, her pulse racing, and she felt utterly confused.

"You sound mad to me," Nana said, calmly.

"Not mad, Nana, confused." Teá realized, though, as Nana was listing off these people, the anger had boiled up. She felt the familiar twinge of guilt, frustration, and anger . . . all of it. Teá, herself, began to wonder. Did she, in fact, have a forgiveness problem?

"I think the incident the other night with Harley was just an expression of your anger at all of these people. You have a lot to forgive, dear. It is certainly not your fault but nonetheless, there are a lot of things that are on you to forgive. So when a little stunt like Harley's the other night occurs, your first instinct is anger. That's not your natural instinct; you are a gracious person, full of love and concern, but when all you have built up inside of you is anger, it is easy for it to spill out on everybody around you."

Nana's tone remained calm, and Teá could feel her love through the line. She wasn't being judged or ridiculed; Nana was just being honest.

"You brought up some people I thought I had already forgiven." A lump in her throat threatened more tears.

"Every time you hear their names or are reminded of them in a situation, you remember everything about them that hurt you." Nana confirmed, accurately.

"I don't understand. I thought I had forgiven them already." Teá generally made an effort to forgive those that hurt her. She thought Todd had been easy to forgive. They were young and dumb, and divorce sounded easier at the time than working through the normal issues in a marriage. Having both girls before either of them were 21 had been a strain, and they'd had some growing up to do, themselves.

The relationship with Adam was short, but ugly. She did not realize she could be so vulnerable to the emotional and physical abuse she had endured. She'd thought she was stronger than that and thought walking away would be easy, especially once it started affecting her daughters. Adam had taken a lot from her: her pride, her confidence, and for a short time, her girls. Forgiveness was not easy. Ignoring the situation, the memory . . . that was easy.

She had loved Todd fiercely, but she'd often found herself making mental notes of his short-comings raising his kids as a single dad.

And Melissa? She didn't even know the woman, but she had caused so much devastation and hurt to these people she loved. She didn't know how she could, or why it would even be expected to forgive her. Now that Teá was more calm as she reflected, she realized there was plenty of forgiveness to deal with.

Nana waited patiently for a moment while Teá quietly considered the people she had listed, but finally interrupted Teá's memories with the true pearl of wisdom. "You think you're mad at Harley, so let's use her as an example."

"Nana, I *am* mad at Harley. It's not that I *think* I am, I really am upset. Nobody else can possibly understand my frustration."

The tears started to fall again. Nobody understood. *Nobody* knew how hard it was trying to parent these children, starting over with Owen, and blending their families. She was angry and she had every right to be mad.

"Who is the one suffering, dear?" Nana softly asked Teá. She seemed to be treading lightly now, not wanting Teá to shut down completely and hang up on her again. "You are the one who doesn't remember what the retreat was about. You are the one who rode home angry and you are the one who didn't get to enjoy the company of ladies form your church. You are the one who is still stewing over it, while Harley is having a good day at school. You're angry, and I get it, but what good is that doing?"

With each pearl of wisdom always came a lesson from Nana. It was like she rehearsed them, had them all ready to dispense to Teá at the first opportunity.

"Being mad at somebody, holding a grudge, and refusing to forgive is like being held captive by your own anger. Imagine taking somebody by the ear and dragging them down into the dungeon, as your anger feels they deserve. You relegate them far away in the recesses of your heart, where no forgiveness, no grace, and no light shines. You have cells there that are built to be strong and solid. You throw past hurts and beliefs about people and their issues into these cells, slamming the doors as hard as you can. While they're there, you believe they can no longer hurt you, but that's not enough. Everybody that passes through this dungeon has to hear about how awful these people were to you— why they deserve to be there.

You have to stay there too, to make sure they don't escape and to ensure you don't miss an opportunity to tell a passer-by all the wrongs your prisoners did. You're bound to get tired down there, standing in the cold and dark, so you make yourself a stool to sit on, guarding and protecting your prisoners and making sure they don't escape. Or worse, what if somebody comes by offering the key of grace to your prisoners? You have to make sure they don't get the key to be freed from the dark parts of your heart.

What you don't see is the rest of the cell, just past where the dim light reflects. You can't see what is on the other side of the bars that keeps your prisoners in their punishment. You can't see the light on the other side where prisoners can wander and carry on with their lives. You can't see the hope being offered. You can't quite make out the green grass, warm food, and the rest of life that is being experienced just outside your vision.

Every now and then your prisoners might come to the bars, hoping that you'll open up and either join them, or at least remove this area from their life, but you stubbornly turn your head, cross your arms, and sit on your stool. The prisoners carry on, just out of your sight. Your anger, your feelings, and all of your emotions are what determines how big this area is for your prisoners. The dark can go deep into their lives and affect many aspects of how they live. Or the darkness can remain a shallow corner in a person's life, not an inconvenience at all. It is possible that your prisoners don't even notice they are in your dungeon.

You are still stuck there in the dark, cold, wet dungeon, though, reminding all the people who pass by of the wrongs your prisoners caused. You are stuck there to make sure the bars don't get released, to confirm that grace will not be offered to your prisoners. I ask, though, who's stuck? Is it *you* or your *prisoners*?

If you allow the hope of grace to open up those bars, the light that is just beyond your sight will start to fill the dungeon again and warmth will start to spread. You can stretch your achy joints, rise from your position as guard, and check out the scenery. You don't have to worry about somebody else freeing your prisoner because you already did. You are no longer bound by the obligation to guard your prisoners; you no longer have to avoid the key of grace.

This might allow your prisoners to have more light in their world and it might give them a little hope of reconciliation as well. If your dungeon intruded into a prisoner's life in a big way, the new light that will shine in that once-dark area will start to bring life and hope again to your prisoner. The grass will slowly begin to grow, the air becoming fresh again. The scars will begin to heal. If your dungeon didn't affect your prisoners' lives as deeply, though, they may not even notice that your dungeon is no longer there. Either way, you are free from your cell too.

That doesn't mean the new area in your prisoner's life is yours, though. It doesn't mean you have to fill that void with your presence. Possibly you will no longer cross paths again, or it could mean the dark places are weak and fragile and you and your prisoner will need to walk tenderly, so as to not disturb the new life. One day it will be stronger and more resilient than ever because it survived the dark. The longer the dark places stay dark, the harder it is for the light to heal them."

Ponderings of a Pearl

1. Nana was quickly able to list all the past hurts that were obviously still bothering Teá. She painted a beautiful word picture of what can happen when you hold somebody prisoner, unforgiven. Can you think of people in your life that you have not sought to forgive?

2. Can you think of a few side effects of being unforgiving that specifically relate to you? We saw that Teá missed the message of the retreat with her friends, and the anger she displayed toward the rest of her family, due to her hardened heart. Can you think of consequences resulting from your own lack of forgiveness?

3. What difference do you think you can make on somebody else's life if you were to work through forgiving them? Remember forgiveness takes two people (you and Jesus), but reconciliation takes three (you, Jesus, and the other person).

4. Read Luke 15:11-32 from the perspective of the brother of the prodigal son. What blessings do you think the brother missed because he was unable to forgive like his father so willingly did? How can you reflect that into areas that you need to forgive?

••• 2 •••

Boundaries

"WHERE THERE IS FRICTION, THERE IS ALMOST ALWAYS A LACK OF BOUNDARIES."

~UNKNOWN

NANA'S PEARL OF forgiveness gave Teá a lot to think about over the next couple of months. Teá was noticing that there was less time to wallow, and she was feeling much better on the weeks that Mia and Ava were with their dad. She noticed that more opportunities were arising to serve at church or to volunteer at both schools (Harley and Lincoln's as well as Mia and Ava's). Also, Teá noticed the more she prayed about forgiveness, the more opportunities arose for her to practice her new-found pearl. Whether they were struggles in her daily life married to Owen or challenges arising from the co-parenting situation with Todd, Teá was noticing opportunities to forgive.

Forgiveness seemed to come easier with each chance to practice. It was like Teá felt a sense of relief every time she let something go, instead of dwelling on it for days or even weeks. Harley was still challenging her authority and Lincoln was still making Teá feel like a stranger in her own home but somehow there was more peace. Teá noticed that things were running more smoothly; she found herself not as angry, and in the few times she did get angry or frustrated, she would recover quickly. She was able to more effectively pray through the issues and move on, which everybody in her life noticed, especially Owen. It seemed as though he wasn't walking on eggshells any longer.

The black pearl was added to her collection of the many others that came before it and she thought about that pretty pearl often. Teá thought it would be beautiful on a string of white pearls. The contrast would be striking. Owen liked it too. He thought that it would be prettier as a single pearl standing alone in its own special setting, like a ring, or on a beautiful chain for a necklace.

Part of practicing her new found pearl of forgiveness was that Harley and Lincoln's mom, Melissa, started to show up more often for time with her kids. This new development added more friction in their home. It was especially challenging for Teá to take steps to forgive her and to find the hope the new pearl brought. Melissa had not been a consistent part of the kids' lives for a long time. Shortly after Owen and Teá got married, Melissa's phone calls became less and less frequent. The scheduled visitations came and went with no word from her. Teá was always there for Harley and Lincoln and once Melissa disappeared out of their lives Teá felt the need to comfort them and show that she and Owen were going to be there constantly and consistently for them. She determined to show the kids what a successful family and a committed marriage looked like.

Teá didn't understand what Owen ever saw in Melissa. The few times she saw her she was less than impressed with her distant attitude toward the kids and her meanness toward Owen. When they talked of their past Teá was shocked at the way Melissa had treated Owen and she hurt for the way his marriage had ended. Teá was even petty, at times, comparing her physique and body type to that of Melissa's. She couldn't understand how Owen could be attracted to two totally different people.

While Melissa and Owen didn't ever quite have to co-parent their children, the few instances they had worked together usually ended in disaster for everybody involved.

In contrast, Todd and Teá always got along great. For the girls' sake their schedule was easy and they both simply did what the girls needed. There were disagreements, and divorce had taken its toll on all four of them but co-parenting with Todd came naturally. Owen was great with Teá's kids and Teá even enjoyed Todd's new wife. She'd rather talk with her regarding the girls than Todd himself. A better relationship with Melissa was needed, but Teá was surprised when after two years, Melissa had showed up one day for her time with Harley and Lincoln.

Naturally, this turn of events created an interesting day. The doorbell rang at 5:00 p.m., sharp. Harley ran to answer, and there stood Melissa. Harley immediately jumped into her mom's arms, and Lincoln came running too. Mia and Ava were curious as well and made their way to the front door to see what all the excitement was about. Owen and Teá were in the kitchen getting dinner started, and slowly made their way to the door, with questions for their surprise guest. Emotions Teá would have felt months earlier, anger, rage, frustration, and confusion, all tried to take root in Teá's thoughts. Instead, her mind almost instinctively wandered back to the last pearl she had received from Nana just weeks before—*Forgive*. Without a second thought, she invited Melissa into her home.

It was the same house that Owen and Melissa had shared but Teá had worked hard to make sure it felt more like her home than Melissa's. She changed the colors, upgraded furniture, and remodeled the kitchen and master bathroom before the wedding. It was her way of making the house hers, as opposed to Owen and Melissa's. Melissa hadn't been in the house since she and Owen had split up, five years earlier. She appeared nervous as she accepted the invitation and stepped in.

Owen told all four of the children, who were now standing back with amazement and curiosity, to go upstairs and finish homework before dinner. Harley started to argue, but one look at her dad shut her up quickly and she grabbed Lincoln, pulling him away from his mom. Ava and Mia didn't even turn around but ran ahead of the other two kids.

Melissa seemed almost embarrassed as she said, "I'm sorry, I didn't call, or warn you guys or anything. I thought the best option was for me to simply show up for my time with the kids. I didn't know what else to do." Melissa was visibly shaken, uncomfortable with her situation. Any confidence that it took to come to the house was apparently gone. She looked like she might suddenly turn tail and run.

Owen was turning red. Teá could tell he was ready to explode at his ex-wife. Teá imagined he was fuming over her nerve to just show up out of the blue and expect to take the kids to who-knew-where. The tension in the room was practically unbearable and Teá felt the heat rising from her infuriated husband. She could almost see the cogs turning in his mind, with everything he wanted to say, but Owen wasn't the one with the temper. That was what Teá was known for. Surprisingly, she remained calm, and through the confusion was the first to find words for Melissa.

"I respect that you're their mom, Melissa, but you cannot just show up like this. Where have you been? You haven't called, you haven't had your visitation, and you can't just. . . just...show up!" Teá wasn't necessarily angry, but she did want some explanation for the unexpected visit.

Melissa sheepishly responded, "I didn't know how to come back, and I wanted to. I want to see the kids; they've grown so much. I want to be involved again. I know there is nothing I can do to make up the time lost, but I want to be able to develop a relationship with my kids again." Her voice was soft, almost a whisper, and she took her time to find the right words as she spoke. She knew the delicate situation she had entered. Teá almost felt sorry for the confused woman.

Owen couldn't hold it in any longer. He practically spit out the words. "Of course they've grown, Melissa, it's been years since you last saw them. Do you even know how old they are? Do you care how they're doing in school, what sports they play, what plays they're in? Do you know anything about these children? No! Get out of this house now."

Melissa started to cry and Teá jumped in. "Wait, Owen, maybe we can schedule a different time to chat with Melissa, once we've all calmed down."

Owen looked at Teá, confused. "Are you taking her side?" Owen spat the words out. Melissa nervously ran her hands over her knees, and Teá wondered if she was wiping the sweat from her palms, or if she was coaxing her legs to stay, not run.

Teá reached out to grab his arm to prove to Owen she was always on his side, and tried to argue her case, "No, I am not taking anybody's side. I think we all just need to calm down, then meet, and come up with a plan so Melissa can see the kids and spend some time with them, maybe even supervised for a while, so everybody can get to know each other again."

Teá called the kids back into the front room, and Melissa said a quick goodbye to them, with a promise to return again soon. Owen and Teá exchanged a glance that said, "We'll talk more about this later."

The evening routine felt strange. The kids were hard to settle after the excitement of the visit. They were busy with their homework, dinner, bath time, and bed routines, but they couldn't calm down. Harley kept asking Teá when she would see her mom again and when it was time for bed Harley made sure to give Teá an extra tight squeeze. Teá thought it was because Harley was afraid to hurt her feelings, wanting so desperately to see her mom, but not wanting to betray Teá. Lincoln was confused. He was sad when his mom said good-bye, but he settled pretty quickly into bed and was probably off dreaming about whatever it is that little boys dream about, before his head hit the pillow.

The entire evening the tension between Teá and Owen was strong. The mention of Melissa's name used to be enough to raise Teá's blood pressure, and ruin her whole mood, but she was just as shocked as Owen when she found herself extending grace to her. Harley's blabbing on and on about her didn't bother Teá the same way it used to; she found herself more protective than offended. She wanted to protect Harley and Lincoln from getting hurt again but she didn't feel anger toward Melissa, or the typical feelings of uncertainty and jealousy when her name was brought up in her house. She rather, felt a little sorry for Melissa, and found herself as curious as Harley about when they would be able to see her again.

Owen was not in a forgiving mood; grace was the furthest thing from his mind. After the kids were in bed, Teá made some tea and carried it to her husband, along with a small velvety bag containing the black pearl. Teá thought Owen needed the reminder. She gently dropped the bag into his hand and folded his fingers over it. He knew what it held; they had discussed it enough. She set the second cup of tea she had been juggling down on the table next to him. He had dusted, vacuumed and arranged everything in the living room prior to plopping himself onto the couch. She folded her legs underneath her as she sat down next to her husband, her own tea warming her hands. For once, Owen did the talking and Teá listened.

"She can't just disappear for years and return with no explanation," Owen began, calmer than Teá had expected. "She probably won't even come back; she never does. When things get hard that's what she does—she leaves. If she does come back, how are we to trust that she won't leave again and break their hearts?"

They both sat quietly, knowing the question didn't need a response.

"She owes us so much: time, money, and explanations," Owen continued after a long silence.

Teá thought about what Owen was saying, and understood where he was coming from, but she could not get past the fact that, as a mother who would give anything to see her children, she could not keep another mother from having time with the children she had borne. Teá knew Melissa was capable of hurting and confusing Harley and Lincoln. She knew that, at times, she and Owen had struggled financially, and it would have been nice to have some help raising the kids. Teá also knew that she had to extend grace. Teá knew that is where peace came from; she had witnessed it time and again in the last few months since receiving the pearl Owen was now running through his thumb and forefinger as if to polish the black away. Teá knew grace and peace were going to come from this, but she also knew that decision was her husband's. She found herself hoping for peace for Owen.

She unfolded herself from the couch, kissed Owen on the forehead, and went to bed.

• • •

Owen was wrong about Melissa not showing up again. She agreed to start with supervised visitation—meeting Owen, Teá, and all the kids a few times for dinner. She even came to their home for dinner with the whole family. Teá tried to remain neutral with Melissa so that Owen couldn't accuse her of taking sides again. Owen needed to see how committed Teá was to her marriage, and the fact that he would accuse her of taking anybody's side hurt her. Despite that, she began to really like Melissa. Things were looking up for the kids as well. They were excited their mom was around more, talking almost daily on the phone with her, and asking when the next time was that they could see their mother.

There was plenty of opportunity for Melissa to start building trust with Owen and the kids. She sounded excited when Harley shared her volleyball schedule with her, and she started making it to most of the home games. They learned that Melissa was out of the relationship that had left her so removed from the children; the man she had been unfaithful to Owen with had pulled her away from most of her family; her children were no exception. They were encouraged that she had a great job, for the first time in years. Owen even received a child support payment and Melissa asked if there was anything she could provide for the kids. She was situated in a nice apartment and was trying to gather appropriate beds so the kids could come stay over some nights.

Everything seemed to be going fine. The peace Teá had noticed before Melissa's arrival seemed to be growing deeper. They were beginning to settle into a regular routine and the kids were all thriving, but Teá couldn't help but notice an unnamed tension between Owen and her. It seemed like she was waiting for the "other boot to drop." She couldn't quite pin-point it, but it made her feel uncomfortable—maybe like she didn't belong there. While the future looked hopeful, Teá was uneasy, like there was an unspoken hopelessness that still remained.

● ● ●

Teá was talking with her pastor's wife one morning and almost accidentally, admitted to her, "I'm tired of feeling like a stranger in my own home." Her friend, Jenni, was interested but confused at Teá's confession.

"What do you mean? I thought you had moved in and made everything comfortable, not only for you, but for Mia and Ava also."

Jenni was right, of course. In fact, just the previous week-end was spent re-arranging and re-organizing all of the girls' things. With all three girls sharing a room, the space was getting crowded and messy. It was bugging everybody, especially Teá. So Owen and Teá bought new beds, new comforters and sheet sets, and some organizing bins to bring a little more structure to the chaos, and give all three girls the chance to have a say in their own room. It'd taken a little time, and as they grew they would continue to need different spaces, but everybody was excited about the new arrangement and Harley even mentioned that it felt empty when Mia and Ava were with their dad.

Teá knew that Owen wanted her there, but with Melissa around so much, she couldn't help but feel like the home wrecker. Seeing some of the interactions between Owen and

Melissa, the familiar conversation, and the ease of discussion about the kids, Teá would find herself wondering, *If it weren't for me, would Owen and Melissa be a real family?*

The thought was ridiculous; Melissa and Owen's divorce was final well before Teá met Owen. Melissa was unfaithful in their relationship and she had made it quite clear that she no longer cared to be married to Owen. Also, Melissa wasted no time moving in with another man well before the divorce was final and custody was arranged. Owen had a history with Melissa, and that was all.

More than that, Owen loved Teá, despite his previous belief that to love again was impossible. He told Teá often how thankful he was that she loved him the way she did. Owen complimented the mother, wife, and woman that Teá was, and Owen was appreciative of everything she did to help their family. Why then, was Teá feeling like the *other woman?*

Teá found herself stewing after a particularly good visit with Melissa. She wondered if the kids would be better off if their mom and dad were back together. She thought about their future and what that would look like if Teá got out of the way so Owen and Melissa could mend whatever was between them many years before. She wondered often, if there were no marriage between Teá and Owen, if he could work on reconciliation with Melissa—the woman he first vowed to.

Teá didn't know how to explain all of this to her friend. She was finally starting to develop this connection with the pastor's wife, a friendship she longed for. She found herself enjoying spending time with her and that she had the ears of a third party, somebody who wasn't tangled in the web of her new role. Jenni listened to Teá as she explained the custody schedules, how visitations went, and how much in love with Owen she was. Jenni smiled and laughed and asked questions. It was like a breath of fresh air to finally make a friend after her marriage. Jenni was also the one who encouraged

Teá to get out and volunteer, to help with the church, and to quit holing herself up in her house. Jenni offered Teá hope.

Again, Teá was at a loss for words to explain her feelings. She trusted Jenni and knew she would never judge her for the way that she was feeling; she just didn't know how. "Am I the *other woman* in this relationship?" Teá finally asked.

Jenni laughed at her, probably a little too enthusiastically. Jenni knew the love Owen had for Teá. Her husband had married them and there was no question that Teá and Owen were meant to be together. Jenni knew they struggled with blending their families; specifically, she knew how Teá's relationship with Owen's kids was a hard adjustment for everybody, but Jenni knew more than anybody, how much Owen loved Teá. Owen showed and expressed it in everything he did. He obviously had no desire to be with his ex-wife. The commitment was no longer there; the love that maybe had existed was no longer there. Jenni's husband had counseled with Owen during the divorce and Jenni knew how much he had struggled. It was exciting for Jenni and her husband to watch Owen grow through that. Then when he met Teá, both Jenni and her husband knew instantly they would be married.

Jenni's humor in the situation seemed a little rude as she laughed at her friend, but she assured Teá, "Owen loves you; you guys are in the covenant relationship. Maybe you both broke covenants with your divorces, but two wrongs do not make a right. Breaking your relationship with Owen is not the stability the kids need. It is not the example the kids deserve, or in the kids' best interest at all, not to mention you and Owen's best interests; you two love each other. You are *not* the *other* woman, you are the *only* woman."

On the drive home the word *hope* came to mind again. This time, instead of the confusion it had always brought before, Teá began to wonder if there was indeed hope for her and Owen—the kind of hope everybody held to, but Teá had never experienced. This idea, this emotion…whatever it was,

Teá sure hoped Jenni was right, that she and Owen would make this work, that their covenant to each other was solid.

Jenni's words felt honest and Teá knew everything she said was true, but she still couldn't shake the feeling. She prepared to drive home after her coffee date with Jenni. The kids were home alone; Owen was out with the men from church. Harley was in charge and Teá was surprised she hadn't received a million texts asking random things or inquiring when Teá would be home. The few times Harley had been alone with her siblings, Teá could never enjoy herself due to the harassment she got from Harley. She shot quick a text from the parking lot, telling her she'd be home soon. Harley texted right back, and with one text, all illusions of hope disappeared. "Okay, no big deal, Mom's here," flashed across Teá's phone screen.

Teá felt the heat rise as anger brewed. Melissa was in her home? Was Owen there too? Who had invited her over? Had Owen known she was coming and never told Teá? She remembered the dirty kitchen she had left with the dishes from the night before and breakfast piled up on her counter. She suddenly became self-conscious about the pile of week-old clean laundry stacked on her couch, and the messy bathrooms. Oh Lord, when was the last time they cleaned their bathrooms? She remembered the unmade beds and the dusting that hadn't happened in a while. She thought about the laundry Melissa would see and the insight into her world that was unwelcome. The closer she got to home, the more she fumed. She pulled into the driveway behind Melissa's car and immediately dialed Owen's number.

"Hello?"

"Hey, did you invite Melissa over?" Teá shot out in response.

"No, when? Why? Where are you?" Owen was obviously confused.

"I went to coffee with Jenni really quick and when I texted Harley to tell her I was on my way home, she informed me that Melissa was at our house. I'm home now and she is here." Teá could feel the tears threatening. She could not cry. She could not give Melissa that gratification.

"Is she just visiting with Harley and Linc?" Owen hadn't heard the anger and anxiety in Teá's voice.

"I don't care what she is doing; she is in my home uninvited. She is seeing things that I don't want her to see. Why would she even want to be in our home without you or me here? I don't understand. Does she think this is her home again? Is that what you want?" Teá was letting the anger, confusion, and anxiety take over and all reasoning had gone out the window. Owen was currently the easy target for her emotions.

"What? No, that's not what I want. Look, I'll leave now, and I'll be home in five minutes." Owen was confused at the rage he sensed from his wife.

Teá sat in her car, fighting back the tears before confronting Melissa. She backed her car back out of the driveway and sat there, parked in the street, with Melissa's car in the driveway. She wondered to herself if this was how it was supposed to be. Was Melissa the one who earned the right to park in the driveway and Teá was still the guest that was to park on the street? *Great*, she thought, *not only is she in my house, she is parked in my spot.* She got out of the car and walked across the lawn. As she reached the front door, Owen pulled up and parked next to Melissa's car.

As Teá opened the front door, she heard Lincoln call from the living room, "Hi, Teá!"

Teá found the three of them—Harley, Lincoln, and Melissa sitting on the couch watching cartoons. It took her breath away. Usually she supported the relationship these kids had developed with their mom. At the volleyball games Teá didn't mind waiting so that Harley could hug Melissa and talk to her before heading home. She was patient when they talked to Melissa on the phone at dinnertime, holding up the whole family from eating. She didn't say a word when Harley came home, excited to tell her mom about her day, and walked right past Teá to get to her phone. But seeing this in her home was too much. It was almost as though she caught her whole family having an affair. They had betrayed her. Owen came up behind Teá, who was too stunned to talk.

"Melissa, what are you doing here?" Owen asked with a voice that seemed nice, but with angry undertones.

"Harley said that everybody had plans today and she was excited to spend a lazy Saturday morning in charge of the TV. She suggested I come over to see how she rearranged her room, and I stayed, but I let her be in charge of the remote," Melissa answered, teasing Harley with her response.

"But you weren't invited by us." Owen said. This time his anger wasn't disguised as well. "We agreed with supervised visitation, not visitation without us here, and at our home."

"I didn't think it was that big of a deal. You guys weren't around, and I took the opportunity to spend a half hour with the kids. Harley was excited to show me her room," Melissa retorted, as she started to unfold herself from Owen and Teá's couch.

"Kids, I'm going to head out. You guys have an awesome weekend, and call me later." Melissa turned her back to Owen and Teá to hug the kids and Owen glanced over at Teá, who was standing next to him. The hurt on her face was evident. "See you guys later," Melissa said, as she squeezed in between Teá and Owen to make her way to the front door.

Neither Owen nor Teá could say anything in response. They were both stunned at what had just happened. They quietly retreated to their room to discuss the morning's events.

"She cannot be in my home without my knowledge, permission, and presence. I really don't think that's too much to ask. I am supposed to be the woman in this house, and I am the mother in this house. I am the one who tucks the kids in and who helps them re-arrange their room." At that moment, another painful thought shot through her mind. Harley kept calling the room she shared with Teá's girls "her" room, and she invited her mom over to see "her" room. All three girls spent the week getting it just right. They each agreed how the room would be best set up, and they worked hard at organizing the whole thing. Teá remembered her oldest, Ava, complaining that Harley didn't do any of the work, and that she just bossed them around. How dare Harley intrude on her girls' space that way, showing it off to her mom!

Owen tried to gather his own thoughts. He couldn't quite understand why he was the one in trouble over this. He truly had no idea Melissa was coming over this morning, and he didn't know that Teá had left Harley in charge. He didn't mind Teá going out with Jenni, and he didn't think it was too much responsibility for Harley to watch Lincoln for an hour or so, but he thought he should know. "Why didn't you tell me you were having coffee with Jenni?" Owen asked, almost accusingly.

"Do not change the subject, Owen. Your ex-wife was in my home uninvited and you want to know *my* plans?" Teá demanded an explanation from him.

"Look, I didn't know she was coming over. I didn't even know you were gone. I don't understand how this is my fault," Owen retorted, starting to pick up the laundry that was on the floor instead of in the basket.

"It *is* your fault; you married her. You had kids with her. You moved me and my kids into her home. You want a family with her again. I am just an intruder. I am the other woman!"

Teá blasted the last sentence without even thinking. Owen looked up from making their bed, stunned.

"Why are you saying that? The other woman? What does that even mean?" Owen's voice was less accusing now, and more confused.

"I am always second. I was the second to live here, to sleep here," Teá pointed to the bed as Owen finished making it. "When I saw Melissa sitting on the couch with the kids today it just reminded me, this isn't my family, it's hers." With that revelation, the tears started to fall.

Owen went to her and gave her a huge hug, the kind where everything could simply be brought back to normal with squeezes that tightened with every inhale. He held Teá's face, and looked deep into her eyes.

"This is *your* family and *your* home. I am *your* husband. Nothing and nobody will change that."

The kids had a lazy Saturday and Owen finished cleaning the house, knowing that Teá was still shaken up. He had the nervous energy that always lent itself to something productive, usually polishing the floors or shampooing the carpets. The housework had gotten a little out of sorts recently, so he got it all nice and tidy again.

Teá locked herself in their room after lunch, with the guise of taking a nap. She crawled into bed and dialed the familiar number.

"Teá how are things? How was coffee with Jenni," Nana answered, seemingly giddy to hear Teá's voice.

"Coffee was fine, Nana. Thanks for offering to watch Harley and Lincoln. I probably should've taken you up on it," Teá confessed.

"Why's that? Is everything ok?" Surely Harley couldn't have gotten in that much trouble," Nana said, concerned.

"Harley is fine, Nana, but she invited Melissa over while I wasn't here, and she came!" Teá felt more defeated than anything else.

"Oh dear, somebody crossed some boundaries," Nana said, sympathetically.

"What boundaries Nana? I didn't do anything." Teá was too tired to argue after the adrenaline packed morning but she was shocked that Nana would accuse her of doing something wrong.

"Not you, Sweety, not you at all . . . Melissa. You need to put up some boundaries and make sure those boundaries are properly protected." Nana explained.

"I don't know what you are talking about Nana. I am so tired and confused. Maybe I just need a long nap, or a bottle of wine, or both!" Teá didn't recall ever being so worn down.

"Extend grace, Dear. Don't ever lose hope, and reinforce those boundaries. Why don't you take a long bath and a nap," Nana said, encouragingly.

"That sounds like a wonderful idea, Nana; we will talk again soon." Teá laughed to herself, noticing Nana's deliberate brush over the wine idea. Nana never said she was against Teá enjoying a glass of wine occasionally but she certainly never condoned it.

At that moment, Teá was thankful for the big spa tub she had insisted on in the re-model prior to their marriage and moving in. She lit some candles Owen kept in the bathroom, turned off the lights, and sunk up to her nose in bubbles. Teá knew the point of the bath was to unwind, but her thoughts were racing. Why did she feel so pushed out of shape when Melissa showed up again? Why was she constantly wondering where her place was in this family? Were things ever going to be normal again—familiar? Who was she even mad at? Was it Owen, Melissa, Harley, or all three? How in the world was she ever going to get through this? Was there hope for them? There was that word again. What did that mean, hope?

When she got out of the tub, there was a cup of tea with a simple note, "I love you," on her bedside table. She sank under the covers of the nicely made bed, and fell fast asleep.

Teá woke and the room was dark. Surely, she hadn't slept that long! She looked at her alarm clock—7:02. Wow, a 4-hour nap! That was completely out of character for Teá. Typically, she slept 30 minutes at most. She worried about being able to sleep that night. Still groggy and a little cloudy, she walked out into the kitchen in her robe. There was a nicely made table, only lit by candlelight. Owen stood at the counter putting the finishing touches on a plate.

"I thought you'd never wake up. You gave me plenty of time to prepare this, though." Owen said with a smile, carrying two plates to the table.

"Where are the kids?" Teá asked, confused more than concerned.

"Nana came and got them shortly after you laid down," Owen answered.

"For how long?" Teá was concerned she had slept through their opportunity for a date.

"All night. They packed over-night bags. Nana said she had a special treat planned and declared there would be no arguing from me. She even gave me the money to buy our dinner and she left this for you." Owen handed Teá a small wrapped box. "And this." Owen found an envelope under his plate and handed that to Teá as well.

Teá opened the gift first, always one to ignore the etiquette of reading the card first. When she took the lid off of the small box, it took her breath away when a pearl that seemed to be made of gold shone up at her. It was on a cotton background, so it stood out exquisitely. Teá couldn't help but wonder if this particular pearl of wisdom from Nana was going to be extra special, due to the gold being reflected from the pearl. She held the box out for Owen to see. "Wow, I didn't know there were gold pearls!" Owen exclaimed, as he lifted the pearl out of its box. There was a sliver of paper under the cotton. On it was written the word Nana had said to Teá hours earlier on the phone: *Boundaries*.

This must be the pearl of wisdom, Teá observed, opening the envelope. Sure enough, there was a long letter scrawled in Nana's beautiful handwriting.

Teá began to read the letter out loud to Owen.

● ● ●

"Boundaries come in all sorts of shapes, sizes, and colors. They can be flexible or rigid, real or imaginary, spoken or not clearly defined. They are there, though, whether you acknowledge them or not. You need to be responsible with and for your boundaries. When there is friction, it is almost always caused by a lack of boundaries. Lack of boundaries in any relationship begs for problems. Boundaries are what make us look at a couple and think, *She walks all over him*, or look at another parent and think, *They need to set some discipline in place for that child*. A life without boundaries is asking for failure but a life too strict with boundaries never allows room for learning. It is a fine line.

"Certain boundaries are smaller, less enforced guidelines that are flexible and can be negotiated. Boundaries we set with our children are flexible, and should always be re-considered as they grow. There are certain boundaries, though, that are strong and impenetrable. Under no circumstance are these boundaries to be crossed. These boundaries are those that protect our relationship with Jesus Christ, and those that protect our marriage, the relationships we hold most dear.

"Boundaries must be communicated. Nobody knows what your personal boundary limits are unless they are communicated. Sometimes new events arise that suggest new boundaries. Sometimes the boundaries define themselves.

"This usually comes with tension, which can be avoided. When a boundary is forced to define itself, it's like a game of Red Light/Green Light. One person is going along just fine, with a green light, and all of a sudden, the other person in the relationship hollers, 'Red light!' The person playing the game starts over and carries on with a green light. This time, maybe 'Red light!' is hollered sooner. Each time the 'Red Light!' command is given, the boundary becomes clearer. The problem, though, is that every time the person who is yelling

'Red Light!' has to holler, friction occurs. The person needs to explain in the beginning, 'If you go past this point, I am upset. You can wander all you want. You have a green light until this point right here,' the friction can be avoided all together.

"Communication is key in boundaries. If you have a strong boundary up, and it is designed to never be crossed, you must explain it to those that might have the opportunity to cross it. You must explain why the boundary exists, how it makes you feel when it is crossed, and why it is so important not to cross it.

"A small warning about boundaries, though: sometimes there are picket-fenced boundaries that are easy to cross, where a strong, reinforced, barbed-wire fence should be and sometimes the strong boundaries that are designed not be crossed ever, should be more like picket fences. It is vital to clearly define these. Boundaries with barbed wire and high fences are meant to protect what is most precious to us. Whether it is a relationship or a feeling we are guarding. Aside from our relationship with Jesus Christ, our marriage is the relationship with the strongest boundaries. These boundaries need to be communicated, re-enforced and communicated again. This is no place for a picket-fenced boundary, which is easy to sneak through. This is where double protection is necessary. It is time for you two to establish some marital boundaries."

Ponderings of a Pearl

1. Melissa was an obvious intrusion on Teá and Owen's marriage. It had to be uncomfortable for them both to allow Melissa to come into their lives, but it was necessary. Enforcing boundaries with Melissa was vital for Teá and Owen to be more secure and happy in their marriage. What area of your relationship needs some boundaries? Where do you feel tension lies?

2. Can you relate to the game Red Light/Green Light that Nana used to depict the idea of boundaries? Have you felt frustrated at times because somebody should have yelled, "Red light!" prior to your crossing a boundary? What boundaries have you discovered by accident, through tension, that you wished would have been better communicated?

3. Are there some areas in which you should have yelled, "Red light!" but didn't, and now you feel like a line has been crossed or a boundary has been overstepped?

4. In the Old Testament walls were built on a regular basis. These walls were the security necessary to defend the community. Some walls fell easily when attacked. They weren't reinforced the way they should have been, and victories were won by invaders, like when the walls of Jericho fell. Other walls seemed impenetrable and were successful in providing the security that was needed. Do you have walls that need to be prayed about, maybe that are too rigid and need to come down? Do you have walls or boundaries that need better reinforcement?

... 3 ...

Protecting the Most Important Relationship

"So it's not gonna be easy. It's going to be
really hard; we're gonna have to work at
this everyday, but I want to do that because
I want you. I want all of you, forever,
everyday."

~Nicholas Sparks, The Notebook

OWEN RUBBED THE back of his neck. He was working late . . . again. He had just hung up the phone with Teá, explaining the looming deadline from his boss. Her flat, dull response to his call confused him. Why was she so frustrated with him? Wasn't it good to call and let her know? Why was missing dinner again such a big deal? He'd be home soon.

His eyes glazed over as he tried to focus on the numbers in front of him but the conversation with Teá kept repeating itself in his head. The last few months had been great, or so he'd thought. The two new pearls from Teá's Nana had given them a lot to think about and work on. It seemed the pearls brought them closer together. Yes, Melissa's sudden return started out rocky, but they had established firm boundaries.

Owen shook his head and ran his fingers through his hair, trying once more to focus on his task. Instead, his thoughts took another turn. He groaned as he recapped how much he had already learned about grace. Admittedly, the concept of grace came more naturally to Teá, but surely she could see he was making an effort. Why would she complicate things now, when everything was going so smoothly? Couldn't she see that his affection, extra work, and thoughts were for her constantly? It felt like she was looking for a fight.

• • •

Owen stood up, walked around his desk, and sat back down, determined to master his swirling thoughts and make some progress on his project before going home. This new job opportunity meant more money for their budget and even though they had a little extra money from Melissa's child support check, it was not nearly enough to provide the children with opportunities Owen and Teá wanted for them. Again, his mind drifted as he thought about the mounting stress of braces, school activities, and the travel team Mia wanted to try out for. When this opportunity had come at work, Owen felt it was exactly what he needed to feel strong and supportive to his blended family. He wanted to be their hero. He sighed and dropped his head into his open palms. Teá knew this would mean longer hours and less together time. She knew the new job was going to come with more responsibilities. He had communicated all of that to her before accepting the position.

Teá had started picking up some waitressing shifts, too. She was enjoying the added interaction she had with adults outside the home. The restaurant was a pleasant work environment and her schedule was flexible. This allowed her to accomplish all her morning routines and still be home most afternoons. She also felt a sense of self-worth and accomplishment as she contributed to the family budget. For the first time in their married life both Owen and Teá were working. The routine of their new jobs complimented the start of a school year, so they were all adjusting to the new rhythms that came with the season.

This new dynamic in their home and family created opportunities for both Teá and Owen to practice their new-found pearls from Nana. They were learning to extend grace when dinner was fast food . . . again, or when piles of laundry seemed to gather dust due to the lack of movement. Throughout each day, they would try to touch base about which boundaries needed to stay and which ones needed some wiggle room. For example, Melissa could no longer determine if, or when she would see the children. Harley and Lincoln needed stability in their interaction with her. Since Harley was in volleyball and Ava and Mia were in soccer, they needed a smoother routine with firm guidelines. With all the chaos that came with the new schedules, Melissa needed to show some stability, and setting boundaries encouraged responsibility.

Owen's mind was a blur as he replayed all of his life's new events over and over, looking for a solution to help Teá see how unreasonable she was being. Sure, he'd like to spend more time with her. This season was simply not conducive to date nights or the alone time that Teá kept wanting from Owen.

• • •

Owen slapped a hand on his desk. The report his boss wanted him to expedite was jumbled numbers in front him; his lack of focus was making this an even longer night. Owen was already stressed and now, after the phone call, he was beyond his limit. He felt like he was doing better with communication; at least he called this time.

He made the seemingly unforgivable mistake of not calling her last Saturday. He had stayed a little longer at the bar than expected when the game went into overtime. She was always angry if he came home late without calling. *This time I call and she's still mad ...can I never get it right?* He reflected on the events of the day and could not figure out why he was going home to an angry wife.

Today had been a normal day; he was busy at work, in and out of meetings. He had checked his cell phone periodically to see Teá's texts but they had contained nothing that needed a response, just informational things about her day. Harley remembered her homework but forgot her lunch. They needed to add money to the kids' meal account and Teá had a busy lunch shift at the restaurant. He read them but didn't see the need to respond. There were no questions that needed to be addressed and he appreciated the communications from his wife.

Feeling defeated at work and at home, Owen saved the document he had been working on, and closed the computer.

He climbed into his truck. As he was putting the keys into the ignition a familiar ring tone signaled he had a text.

"It's Thursday. Where are you?"

Owen had forgotten it was Thursday, and had almost missed the gathering with the guys that happened every week. They met at the sports bar in town where Teá worked. It was the same one where he had stayed late last Saturday. He opened his phone and texted his response.

"Be right there."

He quickly pulled up Teá's number, and texted her.

"I forgot it was Thursday, I'm just going to stop by the bar for a second. Go ahead and eat without me."

Teá didn't respond, so he drove to the small-town bar where the generations of men had been meeting for seemingly decades. It was a comfortable sports bar. Owen rarely drank; but it wasn't about the beer or alcohol. This meeting was more about camaraderie with the guys. They shared weekly news and town gossip. Often, tears were shed over friends who were no longer there, pictures of babies and grandbabies were passed around, and stories of baptisms and graduations sprinkled their conversations. These events were shared amongst Owen's closest friends.

Owen attended a Bible study once a week and he often laughed at the irony. He and his friends either met at the bar or at Bible study. Sometimes, to justify it in his own mind, he felt the need to remind people that the bar was about people, not alcohol.

All the rest of the guys were older than Owen and they helped him in ways for which he never could thank them enough. They stayed by his side and offered fatherly wisdom as he went through his divorce with Melissa. They cheered him on with excitement as he shared the stories of his dating relationship with Teá, and they were all present when Teá and Owen exchanged their vows. They were always there on Thursdays, eager to share in their lives. They were like father figures more than friends, but nonetheless, these were his people.

He walked into the bar and announced that he couldn't stay long. He explained that Teá was already mad at him for working late but he wanted to stop by to see how everybody's week was. The conversation was comfortable. They talked about the upcoming game on Saturday and the loss last week. They talked about the new coach and wondered if this was *the year*. Briefly, each guy updated his drama at home, life with the kids, and his boss. They talked about nothing and at the same time everything in the short half hour. He paid for his cola and another round for the guys, and hurried back to his truck. "Say hi to Teá and the kids, Owen," was the last thing he heard from the crowded restaurant portion of the bar.

As he came around the corner to the house, Owen noticed Teá's SUV was not there. He wondered where she had gone as he pulled his truck into the driveway. He reached for his phone, and texted, "I just got home, where are you?"

A few minutes later, as Owen was taking his shoes off in the bedroom, Teá texted back.

"I took the kids out to eat. I'm tired of being at your beck and call with these kids. I have no help, no support, and I'm tired. I didn't feel like cooking only to enjoy dinner alone without you, again."

Owen was furious! How dare she? It wasn't like he purposefully worked late. The clock in their bedroom read 7:15. She rarely had dinner ready before 7:00 anyway. What was the big deal? He was home. Before he noticed what he was doing, Owen was in the kitchen starting a sink full of hot water to clean the dishes that were left in the sink from the morning before. After the dishes were scrubbed, he moved on to the laundry, starting a load in the washing machine before sitting down on the couch to fold and sort the mountain of clean laundry that always seemed to end up there. By the time Teá and the kids had arrived home at 8:00, most of the clean laundry had been folded, the kitchen was spotless, and the vacuuming was nearly finished.

• • •

Owen didn't like to fight with his wife. In fact, he hated confrontation of any sort. Teá came into the house with the kids and an obvious grudge. She didn't acknowledge any of the cleaning, but went about her regular routine of getting the kids settled in for the night. After making sure lunches were prepped and ready to go for the morning routine, Teá headed to the bedroom. Owen let her do her own thing because he did not want to start the fight that was sure to come. He was furious that she was being unreasonable but kicked himself for not starting a conversation. By the time he crawled into bed Teá was fast asleep, but the house was immaculate for the first time in weeks.

• • •

Friday morning did not bring much conversation between them, just the necessary communication of running a family: no niceties shared, no goodbye kisses, or flirty texts. They each merely went through the routine of their day. The upcoming weekend was rare, all the children would be with their other parents, and Owen hoped to take Teá out for the evening.

At work Owen sent an email to his boss asking if it was ok if he ducked out a few minutes early in the afternoon. Just before 4:00 he sent another message to Teá letting her know of his plans. He was cautiously optimistic that this evening would reset their frustrating course of miscommunication, or rather, lack of communication. Either way, he left the office in anticipation of seeing Teá and enjoying an evening with just her.

Teá was not dressed for a nice date when he got home. She was still in the t-shirt she wore from work at the restaurant, her hair in a messy bun on top her head. To Owen, she was perfect just the way she was. This was the Teá he fell in love with—and he was excited to spend some time with her.

They didn't go anywhere fancy; their favorite sushi restaurant was casual. The atmosphere was relaxed, and the corner booth that they were led to allowed for some quiet discussion amongst themselves. The conversation was light and felt a little like they were avoiding the elephant in the room.

Owen asked Teá if she was enjoying her job at the restaurant and inquired about the new routine with the kids. Teá answered with simple one-word answers, and she inquired about his job as well. They knew that each of them was reluctant to discuss the incident that occurred the night before, for fear of ruining the whole weekend. Teá did mention that she appreciated his help with cleaning the house and Owen lightly apologized for not being more considerate about dinner the night before, but there was no real conversation about the issue at hand.

Saturday was a big day for the Nebraska Cornhuskers, the local team that everybody cheered for. Owen tried to talk to her a little bit about the game. "The Cornhuskers are playing tomorrow," Owen said. "Should be a good game. They're playing a new quarterback that took over when the starting guy got a concussion."

"Mmm, Nana told me. I thought maybe I'd work on that old vanity she gave me. I hate the color. Maybe I'll paint it pink and put it in the girls' room. And I've got to get those drapes over the living room sofa washed. They are beyond dusty. I'd also like to get the pictures hung." Teá's response was less than enthusiastic about the game but reminded Owen of the to-do list she wanted done.

They ate the rest of their dinner in relative silence, got home early, watched a movie, and went to bed. Owen could still feel tension between them, but thought if he left it alone, they would both eventually get over their aggravation.

The next morning Teá seemed to wake up excited about the work she was going to get done around the house, so Owen tried to show interest in her to-do list. He helped her decide where to hang some prints of their latest family photo shoot and together they went to the hardware store to get everything they needed. Teá finally mentioned how thankful she was that Owen had cleaned up the house earlier in the week so she could concentrate on other things that had been neglected. Owen took her compliment as a sign that she was starting to move past whatever was bothering her on Thursday evening, and accepted the words graciously.

The afternoon was turning to dusk, and Owen told Teá he was going to head to Elle's, the Sports Bar where everybody would be watching the big game. All the guys would be there and Owen knew the owner well, having been friends before he was Teá 's boss. He quickly headed into their room to change into his favorite lucky red shirt. When he came out of the bedroom he could almost feel ice coming from Teá. He approached to kiss her goodbye and she walked away without even acknowledging his attempt. Confused, he headed out the door with, "Love ya; see you after the big win!"

As Owen drove the short distance to the bar, he couldn't help but wonder what had happened. They had such a comfortable day together. What had he done wrong? He had told her the night before at dinner that he was excited for the game. He took the time to do the chores she wanted to get done and he could not understand what was going on with her.

Owen walked into the crowded sports bar and found a small table off to the side of the main action. After the chill with Teá before leaving the house, he was not in the mood to be excited and social with everybody. He was determined to watch the game quietly, by himself. The guys briefly acknowledged him as he walked in. They were engrossed in the pre-game show and making their side bets. Owen was caught up in his thoughts about his wife and couldn't get into the hype of the game. Nobody seemed to notice that he had isolated himself.

His distractions didn't last long, though. As soon as the school fight song started playing, the noise from the band and stadium coming through the big-screen TV in the bar, Owen was sucked into the game. He instinctively clapped and yelled along to the rhythm of the song and joined the rest of the occupants at the bar with the chant, "Go Big Red!" Suddenly there was a small sound in the crowd that caught his attention. Nana's voice didn't blend well with the men's voices in the bar and Owen swiveled in his chair to find where it had come from. He was shocked to find Teá's Nana exchanging enthusiastic greetings to all the guys. She was decked out head to toe in the token Nebraska red. She even had a red pom-pom stuck into the back pocket of her red jeans. She greeted each one of Owen's friends like they had known each other for years, asking about their families and giving them all a hard time about how much beer they were drinking. Each person welcomed her, hugging her or shaking hands as she made her way across the bar to Owen.

Owen couldn't find words for Nana. He had never seen her like this, and he was amused to find her here, of all places. He didn't realize that Nana knew his friends and was equally surprised to see how at home she was with them. They made eye contact and she crossed the room to him.

Nana spoke first, "Heya Owen! Big game today. Can't wait to see a Husker victory!"

"Yeah, uh, super stoked too." Owen stammered to recover from the initial shock of finding Nana at such an unlikely venue.

Nana pulled up a chair to join Owen at his small table in the corner and asked, "Mind if I join you?"

"Oh, uh, of . . . course not," Owen stuttered, as he jumped up to help Nana with the heavy chair.

Kick-off had happened by that point and the game was underway. Owen sat awkwardly drinking his cola and sharing a small appetizer with his wife's grandmother. The more the game heated up, the more comfortable Owen grew sharing it with Nana. She was full of knowledge about the team's history. She guessed plays and yelled at the coach and players for missed catches and over-throws. She shouted and ripped her pom-pom out of her back pocket for a victory cheer at each successful play. Owen was still a little shocked at the revelation that Nana was not only a great fan, but the life of the party. A few times after a scoring drive, she ran in between the tables shouting "Goooooo biiiiiiig reeeeeed!" Everybody else would answer in unison: "Go Big Red!" Nana was a ton of fun, Owen realized.

At half time things died down and Nana asked Owen, after shoving a ranch covered French fry into her mouth, "Where's Teá?"

"This isn't her thing, ya know," Owen answered, honestly.

"No?" Nana asked.

"No, you know Teá. She doesn't do football. She doesn't really like to watch the games and she'd just be bored if she were here," Owen explained.

"Oh, so you asked her to join you?" Nana asked, not accusingly, but as though she already knew the answer.

"No, Nana, I didn't. But you know how she is. She'd come because she felt obligated to and be miserable. Or she'd feel guilty for telling me no. It's just assumed that Teá will not come with me to football games." Owen thought it silly Nana would even think that Owen would invite Teá down here for this. Didn't she know her granddaughter?

"Mmm, hmmm, I see" Nana said, even though she obviously didn't agree.

"Nana, seriously . . . can you see Teá down here having fun . . . in this atmosphere? Honestly, I'm shocked that *you* even like to come here, with all the noise, commotion, and nonsense that happens during a game." Owen felt the need to defend himself.

"Look dear, I'm not one to judge, but yes, I can picture Teá down here with you, maybe not enjoying the noise and commotion, but enjoying time with her husband," Nana said, matter-of-factly.

"I wouldn't be paying her any attention if she were here and she'd just grow even more angry with me than she is now. She is already mad at me because I work too much. She gets mad at me because I want to spend time with my friends. She gets mad if I don't text. She literally gets mad no matter what I do. The last thing I want to do is to bring her down here, to be mad at me while I'm trying to enjoy the game." Owen's answer came out more harshly than he intended.

"What does Teá say when you discuss these things with her?" Nana asked.

"I don't," Owen said, hanging his head, a little embarrassed at the emotional reaction to Nana's question.

"You don't? You don't what?" Nana asked, again, as if she already knew the answer.

"I don't discuss these things with her," Owen said, almost at a whisper. "It's just . . . it's just easier if we ignore these things . . . and then they go away. I can't change my work schedule; it's too late now. I already accepted the raise. I don't want to give up my time with the guys after work occasionally. I feel like I'm doing my part in the relationship. Just last night I took her out, and we had a nice evening together. I don't understand what else to do." Owen was growing more and more frustrated as the words spilled out.

"I work all the time; I provide a nice living for us, all of us. I think I'm a good, attentive dad and I feel like we have overcome many obstacles in the short time we've been married, but I feel like every time I turn around she's upset that I'm doing something else wrong. Last night's date was awesome. I am so excited to have her by my side; she's exactly what I've always dreamed of in a spouse." Owen didn't want to admit that the date was awkward, but everything else he told Nana was true.

"And what does she say to this? Have you shared that with her?" Nana repeated the question.

"We haven't discussed this either, Nana." Owen admitted, looking down.

"Owen, if this is ever going to fix itself as you desire it to, you have to address the issues. I am hearing a lot of things that you are doing, and I appreciate the way you can provide for my granddaughter and great grandchildren. I respect that you work hard and that you have relationships outside of the home." Nana placed her hand on Owen's arm. "But, until you start *talking* about the struggles you are having in your relationship, things are never going to get better. Neither of you are mind readers; neither of you know how the other is feeling. Talk to your wife, Dear, and you will be surprised to know that the changes she desires will not be that difficult, after all."

The second half of the game started with the Huskers on a tear; they easily scored three times in the first few minutes of the quarter. The bar was complete chaos with the exuberant fans cheering on the team. Nana was engrossed in the game, but was seemingly having even more fun getting the crowd at the bar riled up than she was excited with the game.

Owen was lost in his thoughts. He wondered if Nana was right. How could he talk to Teá without feeling like he was going to be in even more trouble? Was he truly making things worse by not addressing the issues at hand than waiting for them to smooth over? How would he fix this rift between him and his wife? He loved Teá, truly. He adored the woman. Even her casual look on their date made his heart jump. He loved her natural beauty. She was a devoted mom to his two children, as well as her girls, and he respected her for that. He loved the growth he had seen in her over the past several months as they worked to build a stronger relationship, but mostly he loved that she was his wife.

Owen slipped out the side door of the restaurant after dropping some cash on the table to cover the sodas and fries he and Nana had ordered. He hopped into his truck and noticed a small box on the passenger seat—a tiny box, with a "Husker Red" bow tied tightly around it. Owen slipped the bow off the box and opened it. Inside the box was a pearl. It was the color most would expect a pearl to be—perfect white. It was much larger than the other ones he had seen and shaped like a teardrop. Even as he picked it up he was taken aback by its size. He rolled it back and forth between his thumb and finger and wondered how Nana had put this box into his locked truck. He didn't notice the envelope sitting under the box until he placed the box back on his passenger seat. Inside the envelope was a hand-written note with a familiar scrawl.

Protect the Marriage Relationship at All Cost!

You have many relationships and commitments in your life. Some relationships are fun and relaxed, while others are serious. Many of these relationships involve friends, coworkers, church friends, and family. Each individual relationship comes with its own level of commitment and responsibility. These relationships are vital to a thriving and active life. Each person in your life contributes to making you who you are. You have personal goals, desires, and wants. Each of your personal goals is directly affected by the relationships you cultivate and commitments you make. Your relationships can bring you closer to your goals or push you further away. It is sometimes hard to know which ones to put first and which ones to put on the back burner. Each relationship and commitment has its own level of importance. There is, however, no more important relationship, nor a more important commitment, than your marriage. Your marriage comes first, above all else. The only thing that can and should take priority over your marriage is the relationship you have with God.

If there is hope for a marriage to survive, it needs to be put in its proper place. Children, friends, jobs, ministries or church can come before your marriage relationship, if they are not put in their proper order.

Time and energy should never be exhausted before pouring them into your marriage. If things are good, you need to express your gratitude and appreciation in ways your spouse hears, and in ways she or he understands.

No other relationship is established as a covenant with God except your relationship with Jesus Christ and your relationship with your spouse. Cherish those!"

Ponderings of a Pearl

1. Owen was not doing anything wrong, per se. He was working hard to provide for his family and he was in relationships with men that would build him up and support him. Teá was still frustrated, though, and felt insecure in her relationship, in her place in her marriage. Are there areas in your marriage where you feel your relationship is *WORK* second? What can be sacrificed so the marriage relationship is put back into the proper position?

2. What can you do to strengthen your marriage relationship today? When spending time with your spouse, are you listening and engaged? Or do you just go through the motions of another day, another week, and another year?

3. Nana encouraged Owen to include Teá in things he assumed she would not want to be part of. Can you include your spouse in things that interest you so you can pursue hobbies or dreams together? *I do, he declines*

4. Ephesians 5:22-33 depicts a marriage relationship. It is hard to hear words like respect and submit, but they are clearly written in God's word. There is a hard thing for husbands there too, to love your wives like Christ loves the church. While these are strict commands to hear, they are vital in understanding how God intended the marriage relationship. Wives - how can you show your husbands better respect in their roles in the household? Husbands - how can you love your wives better?

...4...

Everything You Do Matters

"EVERY SINGLE THING YOU DO MATTERS. YOU HAVE
BEEN CREATED AS ONE OF A KIND. YOU HAVE BEEN
CREATED IN ORDER TO MAKE A DIFFERENCE.
YOU HAVE WITHIN YOU THE POWER TO
CHANGE THE WORLD."

~ANDY ANDREWS

TEÁ COULD NOT get a conversation out of her head. She was hurrying home to get dinner started before Owen and the kids made their way home. She had a great lunch rush at the restaurant and was exhausted from running around the whole shift. What was burdening her mind was the conversation she had with one of her regulars as she was finishing her shift.

Many of her friendships in this town had come from encounters at the restaurant where she was blessed to be employed. She loved interacting with customers with whom she had developed strong friendships. In addition, she and Owen both felt the financial burden lift a little. The job was flexible enough that she could still be home most evenings with her family, and because she only worked lunch shifts, she could get all the kids to their separate schools before starting her workday.

She and Owen were in a great place in their marriage and she often found herself bragging about her husband. She complimented him often to her regular customers and people from the small town asked her about him as she served them. Since Nana gave Owen the pearl a few months ago, Owen had been more attentive to Teá, and they made some new rules that included date nights. Owen agreed that he would only work overtime if it was absolutely necessary. He no longer volunteered for extra hours to feel like he was getting ahead in his position. They both sat down with the kids and explained the importance of their marriage relationship, so even the kids understood when date night interfered with one of their sports schedules.

Teá had not felt this comfortable and secure in a long time. Owen was doing a great job at making sure her needs were met, and they were both communicating better than ever before. Further, the boundaries in place with Melissa and Todd, and the comfortable routine that they'd all settled into led to Teá's overall happiness and comfort.

It was this contentment that got Teá excited, and allowed her to share freely with her friends and customers the struggles her blended family had faced and overcome. She loved the marriage she and Owen had worked hard to build.

The uneasiness today came from a customer that seemed to have the exact opposite situation as Teá's current circumstance. Shannon, a regular at the restaurant, often came in after her shift at the local hospital. It was before the kids got out of school and Shannon confided in Teá that she hated going home, especially when nobody was there. She was not happy in her marriage and while she loved her kids, she felt trapped—stuck—with their father. Teá tried to listen to Shannon's complaining, or "vent session" as Shannon referred to it, but all the negativity was wearing on Teá.

Shannon often ordered one of the specialty coffees served at the bar and sat talking to Teá while she finished her closing duties. Shannon would stride in, her long beautiful legs still in her nursing scrubs, her hair messy but pulled back. The minute she sat down, her mouth started moving. Her husband seemed distant, almost neglectful of her. Teá often wondered if Shannon's husband even knew where she was most afternoons. Shannon had about an hour between getting off work and picking up her children from the school. There were few customers in the restaurant that time of day; the lunch crowd had left and it was too early for any happy-hour or early diners. Teá didn't mind the company, except she got mixed emotions when listening to Shannon's rants. As Shannon unloaded her frustrations and misery, Teá found herself daydreaming, her thoughts wandering. More than once Teá wondered if her afternoon companion was satisfied about anything in her life.

Teá always made it a point to discuss the good things in her life with Shannon, trying to overcome some of the negativity she felt from her. She tried not to brag or make it seem like she had things better than Shannon, but she did not allow her customer to bring her down or start looking at her life through the gloomy lenses she wore.

It was during one of those conversations, as Teá was talking about something silly Owen and the kids did the night before, that Shannon dropped a bomb into Teá's lap she did not see coming. The words Shannon uttered cut Teá to the core. "I want a divorce. I want to just get into my second marriage, like you, and be happy. You did it and you are so much better off for it. I think I am going to get a divorce," Shannon said contemplatively, and with little emotion.

Teá felt like she'd been hit in the stomach, like all the air had been pushed out of her lungs. She didn't know how to respond. Looking back on the bad years with Todd—how awful the final years of their marriage were, reminded her of some of the harsh words uttered by them both in the process of working through their divorce. Teá recalled the first time she had to tell her girls that mommy and daddy did not love each other anymore. Trying to explain to the two young innocent kids that their mom and dad were not going to live together was heart wrenching for her and Todd. Teá painfully recalled what it was like to pack up Todd's belongings and separate the house, the marriage, and the family they had built. She remembered the lonely nights shortly after the divorce when the girls were sleeping in the beds in their dad's new house, and Teá was alone in the big queen-sized bed in the big empty three-bedroom house. Teá's thoughts went back to the courtroom where a judge decided the fate of a family in which he had no vested interest. She and Todd talked about the kids like they were bargaining chips in a giant game neither of them wanted to play. Right there in the restaurant, Teá relived all of these emotions. She could tangibly feel the hurt, anger, confusion, loneliness, depression and sadness in the years that followed her divorce.

With all those thoughts running through her head, and the confusion that boiled through with those emotions, Teá was at a loss of words for Shannon. She knew her customer was waiting for her to respond, to say something . . . any-thing, but Teá could not put the thoughts into words. Finally, after a few minutes of silence that felt like an eternity while Teá pretended to sweep, and Shannon watched curiously, Teá managed to say, "You have no idea what those years following the divorce were like. Don't ever wish for what I have because you don't know what I went through to get it." The words did not come across as angry, not by any means, but concerned.

As Shannon sat quietly for a minute, absorbing the words that Teá had managed to express, she casually replied, "But at least for you, there was happiness at the end of the tunnel. In my current position, all that is there is darkness."

Teá didn't recall the rest of the conversation. Shannon didn't seem to notice how much her feelings affected Teá, so the conversation easily changed to the next topic. Teá fin-ished her side work, Shannon paid her bill, and they both went home to their families.

● ● ●

Teá pulled absent-mindedly into the garage and gathered up her bag. As she walked into the house she instinctively reached for her phone and dialed the familiar number. The voice on the other end picked up rather quickly.

"Hello?"

"Hi, Nana, I know you're on vacation, but can we talk?" Teá asked hopefully. She knew Nana would understand. Nana always understood!

"Yes, you actually caught me at a good time. In just a few minutes I have got to go, though. We are zip lining through the trees this afternoon." Nana sounded filled with excite-ment, but Teá was shocked.

"Nana, you are going zip lining?" Teá asked, momentarily forgetting the point of her call.

"Yes. What's the phrase your kids always say? YOLO!" Nana and Teá giggled together at Nana's silly use of slang. Once they composed themselves again Nana asked, "What can I do for you? What's going on?"

Teá hesitated for a minute before beginning her rant, not directed at anybody in particular, and not making any sense.

"Nana, I don't know. I am happy with Owen. I am grateful for the marriage and the family we have. I love him so much and I love his kids and that he is so good to mine. It is almost like the perfect family, Nana, like everything I have ever dreamed of." Teá was trying to lead up to the disturbing conversation she had with Shannon earlier, but she felt she was rambling.

"Did you call me to brag?" Nana teased Teá.

"No, Nana, that's exactly it! That's the thing. It took me so long to get to this point in my life. Remember how miserable I was a few months back when I couldn't get over myself to forgive those that hurt me? Remember how ugly it was before I met Owen? I was convinced I was destined to be alone forever. It was so dark, so depressing. Remember Nana, how much I suffered right after Todd moved out? The process of the divorce itself was absolutely awful!"

Teá was speaking rapidly and her voice caught with emotion.

"Now you are starting to depress me, Teá. Of course I remember. Those were some dark times, but you remained steadfast in your hope, and through a lot of prayers and tears, you made it through that valley. Now you are situated high on a mountain top."

Nana wrapped Teá's life experience up in a nice little Biblical lesson and Teá appreciated Nana's version much better than her own. There was that word again . . . hope. What did hope have to do with this?

"Right, Nana; now I am. After all the struggles, all the lessons, heck even all the pearls, now I am on a mountaintop.

The valleys, though, those were miserable. That was an awful time in my life."

Teá kept returning back to the valleys Nana described, but Nana was anxious for Teá to get to her point. "I'm listening, dear, but what is the issue? Why are you bringing all this up now?"

"Nana, there's a girl at my restaurant that is in a pretty dark place in her marriage. Things are not looking up at all. She told me today she wants a divorce because she wants what Owen and I have." Teá didn't know how to continue or how many details Nana had time to hear about, so she left it at that.

"You and Owen do have a marriage to be envious of. You guys have certainly come out of some rough places in order to make your marriage what it is, and I am proud of you." Nana still did not quite understand what Teá was getting at.

"Thank you Nana, I'm proud of us too. I don't want anybody to look at us and think it was easy. I don't want anybody to want what I have, because of the heartache and pain it took to get here. I certainly don't want anybody to tear their family, their marriage apart, in order to maybe one day be where I am today."

Nana was beginning to understand. "You cannot control what other people think or do, Teá, but you can be honest with your friend. Tell her the truth about the ugliness you had to experience in order to get to the point you and Owen are today. You can also refer your friend to some counseling for help, maybe even invite her to church."

Nana was right, of course. Teá knew she couldn't control what Shannon did, how she felt, or what she saw in Teá's life. She knew what she had experienced was not worth being envious of, and if it was lovely now, it had not always been.

"You're right, Nana, I just really need to be her friend. Thank you. Have fun and be safe!"

Nana chuckled as she prepared to hang up the phone. "I will be safe, and I love you, Teá."

"I love you too, Nana. See you soon, when you get back."

● ● ●

Several days passed and Teá tried to change the tone of the conversations she was having with Shannon. Teá confided in her some of the struggles she had endured with Todd, and how sometimes she wished they would have tried harder. Teá admitted things to Shannon that she did not share easily, and Shannon seemed to be a little more open to working on her own marriage, but Teá could tell Shannon was still unhappy. The complaining continued to echo in every conversation.

Teá was at home, preparing for the girls to get home after a particularly rough conversation with Shannon. She was wondering how in the world anybody could be so negative, as she prepared a little snack for the kids. She knew she would have to leave as soon as Harley and Lincoln got home in order to pick up her girls on time. Harley was old enough to stay home but she enjoyed the trips with Teá and usually tagged along. They were in a comfortable routine and Teá enjoyed the time with the kids in the car, even though it was a little inconvenient.

Teá, Harley, and Lincoln drove up to the after-school program where her girls always waited on the weeks Teá picked them up. Teá noticed right away there was something wrong with Ava. She was walking fast and her look was an icy stare. As she got closer Teá noticed Ava's cheeks were stained with tear streaks and she was obviously fighting back more tears. Teá asked Harley if she wouldn't mind moving to one of the back seats of the SUV so Ava could sit up front. Being the oldest, Harley usually staked claim to the coveted "shotgun" position, but she was accommodating, and jumped out. Ava saw the exchange and grumpily slumped into the seat next to Teá. Once in the car, Teá immediately saw her daughter deflate. The tears started coming fast. Her sobs were audible, and her words were incomprehensible. Teá reached across awkwardly and wrapped her daughter in a hug.

"What's the matter?" Teá asked, concerned, as Ava made no move to return her mother's embrace.

The sobs were coming as coughs as this point and Teá was worried Ava might get sick. "Are you ok? Are you hurt? What is going on?"

Ava wiped the tears, took a few deep breaths, and through the last remaining hiccoughs of her crying exclaimed, "I'm fine; can we go home now?"

The ride home was silent. Nobody dared say anything, but all were concerned about Ava. Ava was Teá's oldest and she was always the more responsible of her two girls. She gave Teá a run for her money with her independent attitude and stubborn resolve. Ava was approaching the pre-teenage phase, and at 10, Teá could recognize some of the familiar hormones that Harley was experiencing. Teá tried to let Ava pave her own path. She was always good in school but not great, maintaining a "B" average, and she had a spirit about her that was unlike any Teá had ever seen. So to see her this broken concerned Teá immensely and she could not imagine what could possibly have happened to bring out this kind of behavior in her daughter.

Owen was home before Teá and the kids, but without a word to him, Teá followed Ava into the room she shared with Harley and Mia. The two other girls stayed behind to discuss the day with Owen and wonder about dinner.

Alone in her room, the tears started again—this time not as violently, but just as sad. Teá again embraced her daughter and let her cry. After a few long minutes passed, Teá asked gently, "What happened?"

Ava pulled away from her mom's embrace and propped herself on her bed. She asked through choked tears, "Why'd you have to get a divorce? Why can't you be married to daddy?"

Teá felt like the wind had been let out of her sails. Of all the things she expected Ava to say, this was the furthest from her mind. The girls were so young when she and Todd divorced and they were now in such a good, familiar place. Although Teá had heard this question was commonly asked among grieving children, Ava had never expressed any type of remorse, and these questions were not some Teá felt prepared to answer. Instead, Teá answered her daughter with another question, "Why would you ask that?"

Ava thought for a long time before blurting all of it out in one long outburst, "I can never go to sleep-overs because when I'm at dad's house he wants me there and when I'm at your house you want me to spend time with the family. There was a big birthday party last weekend and I didn't even ask if I could go because you both always say no. I go to the after-school program half the time because dad gets me straight from school, so I miss all the fun stuff. I hate that I have to bring what I want back and forth. I'm always forgetting homework or something, and I have to re-do it. I don't want to live in two houses anymore. I don't want you and dad to be divorced."

Teá was speechless. Of course Ava was right, all the things she mentioned were true, but Teá hadn't thought it bothered her so badly and she assumed Todd didn't know either. If Todd knew these things were bothering their daughter, surely he would have said something to her.

"How come you have never said anything before?" Teá asked, not accusingly, but curiously.

"Because," Ava was getting choked up again, and the sobs were coming harder as she answered, "That would mean I don't love Owen and Kristen. That would mean I wouldn't have them either."

Of course Ava loved her step parents. Teá's heart shattered for her poor daughter, with her loyalties so divided. Teá wanted to fix it for her. She wanted to take the broken pieces of her daughter's heart and sew them back together, one-by-one. She wanted to somehow kiss it and make it better, like she used to when Ava was little and scraped her knee or bruised an elbow. Unfortunately, there was not a quick fix. There was not a bandage to cover up this wound.

Tears were threatening to fall from Teá's own eyes; they were hot just behind her eyelids. She blinked them back because she knew that was not what Ava needed right now. She didn't know what to do but she knew crying wouldn't help.

Teá sat on Ava's bed next to her and wrapped her in a tight embrace. They sat there for a few more minutes before Teá said, "I'm sorry."

Teá didn't know what she was sorry for—the divorce? The remarriage? Ava missing the slumber party? Emotions that her young daughter didn't know how to handle? Her own inabilities as a mom? She didn't know what she was sorry for, but she knew for certain that she was, in fact, sorry.

After a few minutes, Ava declared she was hungry and Teá sent her off to wash up for dinner. Teá took a deep breath and headed down the stairs to her family.

That night, in the dark of her bedroom while Owen was showering, Teá called Nana, who had just returned from her vacation.

She recounted the events to her beloved Nana and listened as Nana prayed for peace over the situation. She sat silently as her Nana prayed for the family, prayed for peace and reconciliation, prayed for a forgiving spirit for Ava, and prayed for hope. After the prayer, Teá whispered, "Amen," and hung up.

● ● ●

Ava seemed to settle down as the week went on but Teá was still recovering from seeing her daughter so shaken, so distraught, over something that Teá hadn't even considered had hurt her. Teá and Todd had discussed the divorce at length and believed the girls deserved to be in a home where love and friendship were the standard, not where fighting and bickering was the norm. They had discussed how their fighting was hurting the girls, but if Teá was honest, they had never discussed working through the issues that caused the negative emotions in their home, they simply discussed divorce as if there was no other option.

Teá walked down her driveway to check the mail a few days after picking Ava up that fateful afternoon. She laughed as she thought of the hormonal pre-teen emotions that she must be dealing with to be so devastated one day, and seemingly normal the next. She wondered if Ava was getting enough sleep and she started to wonder again whether she and Todd had tried hard enough. Not that she would change anything, she and Owen were in such a beautiful place that she truly couldn't imagine life without him, unlike a few months earlier, when she had daydreamed about a life without Owen, or Harley and Lincoln. She couldn't help but wonder "what if."

Teá was surprised when she opened the mailbox and found a little package, with Nana's familiar scrawl written across.

Another pearl, Teá thought. It was strange to be receiving yet another pearl. Nana had been full of her little nuggets lately, but Teá couldn't think what in the world Nana would give for advice with this one.

She carried the tiny box into the kitchen and thought she'd play a little trick on Nana. Before opening the obvious jewelry container, she grabbed her phone, put in her blue tooth so she could cook dinner while they talked, and dialed her Nana's number. "Teá, is everything ok? I am with somebody for a cup of coffee, but didn't want to ignore your call."

Nana sounded fairly frazzled, and Teá could tell from the background noise that she was somewhere crowded. "Everything is fine Nana. I just received a package from you today, and I'm afraid there has been a mistake."

Teá couldn't help but let a smile glide across her face as she spoke louder than normal so Nana could hear her over the noise of the busy shop.

"A mistake? Why?" Nana asked, confused, but also sounding distracted.

"Because...I don't need any more pearls. I have all the wisdom I could possibly need." Teá wanted Nana to be alone so they could discuss the contents of the box, but she also wanted to give Nana her space and privacy. Her sarcastic answer seemed to go unnoticed by Nana, who was obviously preoccupied.

"Hmmm...I don't know, Todd, what are you having? Sorry, Teá I really must let you go, can we talk later?" What? Was Nana with Todd? Was Todd Nana's coffee date? Did she really just say Todd's name? Why was Nana with Todd?

"Nana, are you with Todd? Like, *my* Todd. . . well, my ex-Todd?" Teá stammered out the last sentence. She was speechless. What could Nana possibly be doing with Todd?

"Yes, dear, why?" Nana asked casually, like why would Teá be bothered that Nana was with her *ex-husband* having a coffee date? Why should Teá care that the man that broke her heart all those years ago was impeding on *her* Nana? What was the big deal that Nana was betraying the relationship with her very own granddaughter?

"Ok, well, I'll let you go then." Teá said through clenched teeth.

"Sounds good. Call later tonight, ok?" Nana was clearly clueless about Teá's anger, and that just added to her fuming fire.

Teá hung up the phone and immediately started to cry. Why in the world was this ok? In what universe was it acceptable for *her* Nana to have coffee with Todd? Didn't she know that Todd was the "ex?" Didn't she understand that, while they had worked on forgiveness, that didn't mean they got to be friends? Didn't Nana have any loyalty at all to Teá, to the girls, or to Owen?

Owen. Teá was so angry for herself that she forgot about how this was going to feel for Owen. That kind of betrayal, after feeling so welcomed into Teá's family, felt wrong. Owen was going to feel betrayed by Nana. This new revelation made the tears fall even harder.

● ● ●

That night Owen could tell something was wrong, but he and Teá went about their normal routine. Owen was almost afraid to put the girls to bed because he was convinced a fight would ensue with Teá. He could not, for the life of him, figure out why she was so upset. He kept himself occupied by spending extra time doing up the dishes after dinner. He cleaned out the fridge while the kids did their homework at the dining room table, removing each shelf and hand washing, then drying, and finally placing them back into the fridge. He started on the stove before he realized it was bedtime. He could finish it after tucking the kids into bed, he thought. He replaced the gas burners after giving the stove a quick wipe-down and hollered, "Bed time!" He didn't know where Teá was. She had been sulky and pouty all night, so he was the one giving orders for showers, brushing teeth, and running the bedtime routine.

Putting the kids to bed and declaring one last, "I love you all," Owen closed the door and began searching for his wife. He found her in the kitchen, finishing the job he had started on the stove. He walked in, folded his arms across his chest, and watched his wife finish the job. Of course she wasn't using the correct cleaner, and the wash rag Owen had used for dishes would need to be washed, or maybe thrown out. It amused him that Teá thought it would be helpful for her to do his tasks.

"What's the matter?" Owen asked, after watching her for a few minutes. It startled her and she jumped, spilling cleaning solution all over the counter.

"Ugh! Owen! How long have you been standing there?" Teá was frazzled and trying to clean up the mess the soap was leaving as it dripped down over the bottom cupboards and onto the floor. Owen failed at suppressing a grin. She really was clueless when it came to this stuff. "Long enough to watch you clean the stove with the wrong stuff. It's ok that it spilled. That's what I use to clean the floor."

Owen started walking away, toward the closet where the towels were kept, in order to help his wife clean up her mess.

"What's the matter with you tonight?" Owen had to raise his voice a little so she could hear him as he walked away from her. He wanted her to know he wasn't leaving.

"I talked to Nana this afternoon . . . well, I heard Nana this afternoon. I guess I talked to her . . . I don't know."

Teá was visibly shaken, upset about the conversation she'd had with Nana. "What'd Nana have to say? Did you get a pearl?" Owen knew the arrival of pearls sometimes prompted hard conversations, but he hadn't seen Teá this shaken in a long time.

"Yes, no, sort of . . . but that's not what is the matter. She was having coffee with Todd." Teá appeared sheepish and the remark took Owen by surprise.

"I didn't realize they hung out, or that Nana kept up a relationship with him," Owen said, genuinely curious. His question wasn't necessarily why Nana was hanging out with Todd, but why it was making Teá so angry.

"I didn't know that either, I am sorry she betrayed you like that, Owen."

"Betrayed *me?*"

"Yes, I can't believe she would continue a relationship with Todd, even after welcoming you so warmly into our family."

"You don't think Nana has enough love for us both?"

"Well, of course she does, but Todd hurt me so much. That marriage was a disaster, and he was such a jerk about the girls following the divorce. Nana heard and saw all that he did to me." Teá was getting louder, and Owen knew he was walking on thin ice. Now that he knew it wasn't him she was mad at, he did not want to add fuel to the fire.

"I don't mean to sound flippant about this, but I don't understand why it is such a big deal that Todd and Nana still communicate. She's still the girls' Nana, and she accepted him just as she accepted me."

Teá looked confused. "I expected you to be mad. I am furious."

"I'm not mad, Teá. I don't want to have coffee with him and I have no desire to build a relationship with him but the truth is, he is going to be a part of our lives for a long time and we need to be ok with that. If Nana wants to have coffee with Todd, let Nana have coffee with Todd."

Teá was unrelenting. "You clearly don't understand. I am betrayed."

"I am sorry. I do not understand. Did you get a pearl from Nana?"

Teá's eyes widened, remembering the pearl. "Yes, but I didn't open it. I was going to tease Nana that I didn't need any more pearls, but we were interrupted by the obviously *very* important conversation she was having with Todd. I'm not opening it."

Teá was being ridiculous. Even she could feel her emotions getting out of control, but knew there was no way to stop it. She was furious with her Nana.

"I think you should open it, but I also think we should go to bed."

During the conversation, Teá had forgotten her task of cleaning up her mess, and had perched up on the counter top while Owen cleaned the floor, the cupboards and finally the stove.

● ● ●

The next day, Nana called Teá but Teá didn't answer. She let it go to voicemail and did the same thing the following day. Finally, after three days, Teá couldn't take it anymore. The calls from Nana, the nagging from Owen and the unopened packet on her nightstand got to be too much for her to ignore much longer. When her phone rang, she couldn't resist.

"Hello?" Teá answered, her voice tight and full of anger.

"Well, hello, dear. How are you?" Nana said, in her typical style. She acted as though she hadn't a care in the world.

"I've been better," Teá answered honestly.

"I am sorry if I offended you Teá, but I do have lunch or coffee semi-regularly with Todd. I am not sorry for that." Nana was honest and Teá could feel the tears begin.

"How Nana? Why?" Teá didn't try to stop the anger, hurt, and frustration. She let it spill over into her phone conversation.

"Because, I love him. I didn't like him at first, remember, when you two first started dating? Nobody could be good enough for my Teá. But I watched him become an incredible husband and then a good father to those I love, and I fell in love with him too. I care for him deeply, and it is important for me to spend time with him. I'm surprised you haven't heard about it before. I have actually taken him and the girls to dinner on more than one occasion."

Teá sucked in a deep breath at this revelation.

"The girls know you and Todd are *friends?*" She could not understand.

"Absolutely. They know we hang out at times. Have you opened your pearl?"

Teá was confused at Nana's sudden change of subject. "No, it's still in the package," Teá answered, almost pouty.

"Will you open it now?" Nana asked, knowing she would.

Teá had already been playing with the box while talking with her Nana, and she opened it to find the pearl.

The jewelry box was similar to what you would use for a ring, but inside was a little velvet pull-string bag. Teá opened the bag and pulled out a little note. Written in Nana's scrawl was a sentence: "Everything you do matters, and it matters to a whole lot of people." It was a longer piece of paper than easily could fit in the bag so Teá had to smooth it out before reading it. She held the small bag upside down over her hand and out fell a gorgeous green tinted pearl, this one larger than most she had received from Nana, and it was an oval as opposed to being perfectly round. Teá admired the beautiful pearl for a second before saying out loud,

"Ok, Nana, what does *this* mean?"

"The decisions you made in life affect more than just you in that moment. You have realized this in the last few weeks, with your friend from work who has wanted a relationship like you have with Owen, in the break down with Ava over the divorce, and in my relationship with Todd.

"It is said that when a butterfly flaps its wings across the world, the wind from that wing flap can grow to the point of creating a tsunami on the other side of the globe. That concept is true in our relationships, in the decisions we make every day, in every little thing we do. It is also said, 'Don't sweat the small stuff.' But it is the small things that affect all the aspects of our lives. A decision to end a marriage, to buy a new car, to rent or buy a house, have repercussions that last a lifetime. When you end a marriage, generations are affected; families and extended families are forced to change their loyalties, to evaluate their relationships, and to change their traditions. Children of divorced parents are more likely to divorce, themselves, and so the pattern is in motion.

"Do not make any decision lightly, and understand that everything you do will affect the people around you, possibly for generations to come. You cannot get mad at the chaos you create based on decisions you made. You can, however, explain this pearl to others so they can better understand the impact their decisions will have on those around them, and possibly even on you."

Ponderings of a Pearl

1. What repercussions are you still seeing from decisions made in prior relationships or marriages? Statistics show that children who come from a divorced family have a higher chance of divorce, themselves. What can you do for your children and your family to show the importance of every decision made?

2. Seeing how much each decision affects those around us: our friends, family, co-workers, and acquaintances, should help us consider the little things we do each day. What decisions do you make without thinking, that could affect or influence others around you?

3. While we cannot change what we have already done, we can consider, with prayer, the influence we want to be on others. Our actions and words can hurt or encourage, build up or tear down, affirm or deny somebody else's thoughts, feelings, or emotions. Will this change the way you see yourself as an influencer?

4. Matthew 5:14-16 says that you are a light in the world, a city on a hill. Everything you do matters to many people. Are you reflecting the love and light that you are supposed to, or are you reflecting something else you never intended?

... 5 ...

Pick Your Battles

"Choose your battles wisely. After all, life isn't measured by how many times you stood up to fight. It's not winning battles that makes you happy, but it's how many times you turned away and chose to look into a better direction. Life is too short to spend it on warring. Fight only the most, most, most important ones, let the rest go."

~Unknown

TEÁ COULD FEEL the warm, late summer air on her face. Her hair was going to be completely destroyed by the time she and Nana got to wherever they were going. She giggled every time she thought of Nana insisting on renting the Mustang convertible for their adventure, as Nana referred to their short weekend getaway. They both had vehicles that would make the drive just fine, but Nana wanted an adventure.

They were only a few miles into their trek, the surprise trip that Nana had said needed to happen in a town a few hours away from home, and Teá was lost in thought. She was excited for the two days away that Nana had surprised her with and she was stoked to be having alone time with her Nana. Owen had helped her pack that morning and although he had relieved some of the guilt she was feeling about the trip, promising he wasn't mad, she couldn't shake the feeling she should have stayed home with her family, instead of splurging on a weekend getaway with Nana. While he was following her around the house, helping her gather what she would need, Owen described what he was going to do with the kids. Ava and Mia were with Todd and Owen had a fun ice-cream date planned with Harley and Lincoln.

It was the ice-cream date that bothered her. Teá couldn't seem to shake it. She couldn't understand why he was willing to promote poor eating habits. The food debate had been a fight between Owen and Teá for months now and frankly, Teá was tired of it.

Her own girls had been exposed to healthy eating habits since the beginning; it was important for both Todd and Teá that they establish healthy eating while the girls were young, so they could avoid this fight later on. Now, she was fighting Own and her stepchildren over something she felt was important—being healthy.

Owen had tried his hardest as a single dad before he met Teá but he'd struggled with meals. He knew it was wrong, but too often fast food drive-throughs were the easiest, most convenient ways to answer, "What's for dinner?". Even when the kids were very young, Melissa was not a good cook and she certainly chose what was easy over what was healthy. Through these habits, Lincoln and Harley had become picky eaters and they always turned up their nose at whatever Teá prepared for the evening meal. Teá packed their lunches and let them pick a snack or two that was not the healthiest, but she always made sure to include a protein and vegetable, which were usually discarded.

Dinner was the worst, though. It was important for Teá to cook most nights for her family. She was a meal planner and was consistent with her choices of healthy options for the family. This is where the fighting began. Her stepchildren didn't appreciate home cooked meals. They turned up their noses at any vegetable presented, and they argued in protest when they were told, "This is what is for dinner. You'll eat it, or nothing." They expected both Owen and Teá to jump to their beck and call and prepare whatever they wanted. They didn't take other family members' desires into consideration, they didn't care about nutritional value, and they certainly didn't earn any respect from Teá. Owen, on the other hand, always gave in to them. He would tell Teá, "It really isn't worth the fight. Just let them have some macaroni and cheese or something." Or he would offer them a peanut butter and jelly sandwich when they were not hungry at the dinner table, but were *starving* an hour later.

"It's not worth ruining our night over," Owen would say, justifying his actions with his kids. Teá was relentless though, and often wondered if his thoughts were about Melissa and not actually about the kids. She wondered if Owen was avoiding the conflict with Melissa that *might* arise if he were to take a stand with their children.

It felt to Teá like every time she stood up for something, Owen questioned what Melissa would think. Frankly, she was tired of justifying her actions to Melissa, through Owen. Teá reflected back on the latest big fight with the kids.

● ● ●

Ava, Mia and Harley were all cleaning out their room. With such a small space for all three girls they each had to make sacrifices. Owen had done a pretty good job of keeping it clean and helping the girls establish routines, but it still always felt crowded.

One weekend, when Harley was with her mom, Teá offered to help Ava and Mia organize their room a little better. Teá was surprised to find how many stuffed animals Harley had. They overflowed from her bed and were piled up in a corner of the room, essentially taking up way more space than was necessary, especially since Teá thought it was overboard for Harley, being the oldest of the girls, to have so many. Teá had mentioned to Owen that Harley could pick two of her favorite stuffed animals and the rest had to go. Owen didn't think it would be a big deal for Harley, but they were wrong. Harley threw a huge fit, protesting, "It isn't fair! Why should I have to give up my things? They fit just fine!" She cried, screamed and yelled the entire evening after Teá broke the news to her. Teá stood her ground and did not budge. She felt the number of stuffed animals in the house was out of control. Truthfully, Teá hated stuffed animals. They collected dust and she had an unrealistic fear of spider nests in the piles of fluff that were overtaking the girls' room. Teá was not going to give in on this one. In her mind, Harley was almost 13 years old, and did not need stuffed animals. She didn't play with them. She didn't even acknowledge they were there most of the time. Yup, the animals were going to have to go.

The next morning Harley presented an idea to Teá. Through blood-shot eyes she explained that she could put the majority of her animals in Lincoln's room. The solution was fair, she thought. She could keep her animals and they wouldn't take up as much space as in the girls' room. Teá was still not pleased with the amount of animals and she had already made up her mind. She did not agree to Harley's request, which brought on the temper tantrum again.

Owen asked Teá what the big deal was about the stuffed animals, and Teá felt like she had to defend herself. Owen explained that Melissa also had quite a lot of them in their house when they were married but that solidified, in Tea's mind, the determination that the stuffed animals were leaving.

Again, Teá did not understand why she had to justify her actions to Melissa or Harley. Teá didn't understand why Owen couldn't just take her side for once. These were the boundaries Nana had taught them about; Teá was simply establishing boundaries. She knew from experience that sometimes boundaries came with a bit of friction but eventually things would settle down and be better, just like things were today, with Owen and Teá.

● ● ●

Maybe there was hope for them after all. There it was again . . . hope. Sure, things were not always easy. Sure she and Owen still had issues; forgiveness was a daily decision and establishing boundaries was still a struggle, but perhaps there was hope for their marriage and for their family. Teá couldn't remember the last time she considered what would happen, should their marriage fail. Through a prayer one day at church, she remembered feeling a sense of peace. Owen was beside her, holding her hand as he always did when they prayed next to each other, and she had never experienced that level of peace . . . that level of acceptance, and that much hope.

● ● ●

Teá's mind was still wandering as Nana continued to drive down familiar streets. She remembered all the times she cried to her friend Jenni about how hopeless their marriage was, how hopeless the process of blending their families was. She remembered how angry she was at the entire, hopeless situation. Teá explained to Jenni one time how frustrated she was with her newly combined family and how much like an outcast she felt. Jenni had made the comment, "But God." That comment resonated with Teá as she was finishing up her tasks volunteering at the daycare and she couldn't shake it. It was like Jenni was reminding Teá that there still was hope. Jenni agreed that things were broken then, but God was bigger than any of it. Jenni had seen the damage done and the hopelessness in the situation, but also knew that God was able to overcome it all.

Their marriage had come so far! There was a point in the past where she honestly thought they would not celebrate another anniversary, but she was so happy with him now. It was amazing to her how much could change. Teá reflected back over Nana's last pearl, and how much the decisions she'd made over this year affected where they were right now. Remembering the pearl before that—the one Owen received that reminded him to make their marriage relationship a priority, inspired her to ponder the changes they made when Nana taught them about boundaries. A huge smile spread across her face when she thought how far their relationship with Melissa had come. Melissa was a regular in their family now and she was good for the kids. Teá's heart had changed so much that she was even thankful for her help, considering it a blessing that Melissa was now more involved with Harley and Lincoln. This reminded her of the first pearl she had received from Nana, the first in a long time. The *Forgiveness* pearl—it was almost like Nana knew that one pearl would set off a chain of events leading to the next four.

● ● ●

Teá was brought back to reality when she remembered the ring on her finger. Owen had surprised her by having the *Forgiveness* pearl set into a ring and giving it to her on Mother's Day. She wore it almost every day and it was a constant reminder to her of how important forgiveness is.

As Nana continued driving down the interstate Teá's hair whipped around them both. Nana caught sight of Teá playing with the ring and noticed she was far away in thought. She broke the silence.

"A penny for your thoughts?" Teá hesitated for a moment before answering Nana, and Nana began to wonder if she hadn't heard over the noise of the rushing wind.

"It was a year ago, Nana, almost exactly—since you gave me the *Forgiveness* pearl." Nana kept her gaze ahead, focused on the road.

"Oh, it was? Has it been that long?" Teá twirled the ring around her finger absent-mindedly. She was contemplating the pearl, mulling over what it meant to her.

"Yes, almost exactly a year ago, when Harley and I went to the conference, remember? I was so angry. I was bitter toward that poor girl. Of course I didn't realize how much being unable to forgive everybody in my life was affecting the relationships with those I love most. That's why you gave me the pearl, remember?"

Nana was listening intently, focused on the road. She was pleased that the important lesson for Teá had taken root. She thought the setting of the pearl—the ring Teá was wearing—was a lovely gift from Owen, and she appreciated that he realized its importance. "Of course I remember."

Teá and Nana had travelled the highway a few more miles when Teá interrupted the silence. "I have two questions. I need an honest answer to them both."

Teá was joking with her Nana; she was in a great mood despite the memories of the recent fights with Owen and Harley. She loved the time with her beloved grandmother, but she was pretending to be stern.

"I can promise I will not lie, but that does not mean I will answer the questions." Nana matched Teá's wit with her response, like she always did.

"Question one, where are we going? What are we doing?"

Nana grinned at Teá's questions and didn't miss a beat. "That's two questions."

"Ok, fine, what are we doing this weekend?" Teá responded to Nana's sass with an eye roll as she asked the question again.

"We are bonding—spending some *Nana and Teá* time."

Teá knew Nana wasn't going to relent. She'd been hounding Nana for weeks but that was all Nana would tell her. She knew Nana had something planned, because when she asked Nana if they could do it another weekend, Nana said it would ruin the plans. "Okay, fine. Don't tell me . . . I hate surprises, you know? Question two, how do you choose your pearls?"

Nana smiled and answered, "Now that is a question I can answer, but not for about another ten miles."

Teá looked incredulously at her Nana. "What's in ten miles? Why can't you answer now? You're no good for a girl that doesn't like surprises, no good at all."

Nana and Teá teased each other for the next ten miles. Teá was trying to get an answer out of Nana—any answer. Teá did not have any further information, when Nana suddenly signaled, and took an exit in a strange area that Teá had never noticed before. She had been down this road several times, but hadn't paid attention at all to this exit.

Nana knew exactly where she was going, though—like she had traveled to this destination many times. It was a rural neighborhood—a bedroom community with quaint houses and big yards. Most of the lawns were nicely kept, even in the late summer heat. Some trees had swings hanging from them, and many yards were fenced in because they had dogs. The neighborhood was inviting, each house uniquely designed, without the cookie-cutter feel of some subdivisions. The land was sprawling, and the longer Nana navigated the roads, the more Teá could see the houses occupied larger plots of land. The rush of the wind slowed as Nana decreased her speed to 35 miles per hour. It seemed there was a stop sign at each corner.

The further Nana drove away from the interstate, the more Teá wondered how in the world Nana knew where she was going and how many times Nana had traveled out this way. Teá interrupted the silence occasionally with a question, just checking to make sure Nana knew where she was going. Finally, Teá asked, "Nana, what are we doing? Where are you going?"

Nana smiled, "Almost there. I thought you wanted to know how I chose the pearls."

Teá was even more confused. "And your answer is found out here, in the country?"

Nana's smile grew even larger, "You'll see."

The final statement let Teá know she was not going to get any further information from her Nana so she sat back and enjoyed the quiet drive. The speed limit increased again, and they headed further and further away from the interstate. Teá laughed at the thought that Nana said ten miles and thought to herself *more like ten hours*. They were on a two-lane high-way now and the scenery was gorgeous as they approached a little hill covered in green. Nana slowed down and signaled right at the foot of the hill. She almost drove right past it before Teá noticed the tree-lined driveway. Nana pulled in like she owned the place, until the trees broke, revealing a cute little cottage.

Teá was shocked when she saw the small, humble property. It looked like it came straight from the beach! A netting hung over the exterior wall, along with two round, red and white-colored life preservers. The house itself was painted bright blue and the front stoop was like a boat dock. The windows were trimmed in sun-bleached white, and there was a sign by the door with an arrow pointing to the left, with "Beach" written across it.

"What is this place, Nana?" Teá was in complete wonderment and shock. They were nowhere near an ocean and sure enough, her Nana had parked right outside a beach house.

"Teá, this is where my pearls come from. You wanted to know how I choose my pearls, and I'm about to show you."

Teá's mouth dropped. "Nana, I meant . . . well, I didn't mean . . . Nana you took me to a beach house!"

Nana chuckled and got out of the car. "Are you coming or not?"

Teá slowly unlatched her seatbelt, opened the car door, and started walking toward the little cottage. She could not believe her eyes. A beach house out here in the middle of nowhere?

Nana knocked twice on the door as Teá quickened her step to catch up. The boat dock was long and awkward to climb, but it was the only way to get to the front door.

A man about Nana's age answered the door. He was dressed in a Hawaiian shirt and khaki shorts. He had flip flops on his feet and sunglasses on his head, which was strange, because he had a tan-line from the glasses that seemed to go all the way to his bones—he was so tan, and that area was so light. His white hair was disheveled, and if Teá didn't know better, she would have thought he lived on the beach. He apparently was the resident of this beach house, and a friend of Nana's.

"Joe!" Nana exclaimed, wrapping him in a huge hug. They embraced for a long moment, with Teá awkwardly standing on the boat dock, not quite knowing what to do. She couldn't help but wonder what her Nana had gotten her into.

Joe pulled away from Nana's embrace and looked at Teá. "You brought a guest this time. Who's this?" Joe asked, with a welcoming grin.

"Joe, this is my granddaughter, Teá," Nana exclaimed with a hint of pride in her voice.

Joe grabbed Teá and wrapped her in a tight hug. Teá didn't know how to respond. She didn't even have time to react to his embrace, so he hugged all the way around her, arms and all.

"Come in. come in. I just got back from the farm and I am excited about some of the amazing creations the girls have made." Joe ushered the two women into the house. Nana marched in behind Joe, with familiarity that only comes from a comfortable and longtime friendship.

Teá hesitantly walked through the front door. *The farm?* Teá was thoroughly confused. Joe, apparently the owner of a beach house, traveled to a farm?

Once inside the house, the shock of seeing the ocean décor did not end. The marine theme continued throughout the entire house—at least from what Teá could see. There were beach signs and seashells, sand dollars and sand buckets all over the place. Stuffed sea animals adorned shelves on the wall and signs like *Welcome to Margaritaville* and *No lifeguard on duty* hung on the walls. Teá felt comfortable here but this little place was bizarre.

"Come on in. I was just rinsing them off in the sink when you knocked; perfect timing as always," Joe said, looking at Nana, but addressing them both. He waved his hand, directing them into the kitchen. Nana and Teá followed obligingly. Teá was a little slower than Nana, distracted and soaking in all there was to see in this strange little house that belonged by the sea.

When she passed a wall blocking her view to the kitchen, Teá's face lit up. Her mouth slowly spread into a grin at the sight. There on his kitchen counter, next to the sink, was a spread of pearls. They lay on a black towel so they would not roll around, but the dark terry cloth contrasted with the majority of the pearls. There were probably over 30 pearls spread out on Joe's kitchen counter. She noticed giant oyster shells laid upside down all over the countertops, and in each one were probably a dozen pearls. There were pearls everywhere.

Teá was speechless. She stood in astonishment, taking it all in.

"Joe operates a pearl farm, but not here—at his beach house," Nana said to Teá, as though no other explanation was needed.

"Oh, his, beach . . . house," Teá said, unable to hide her confusion.

"Not *this* beach house is what your Nana really meant to say." Joe chuckled, knowing full well the irony of the statement Nana just made.

Teá had many questions but she knew it was inappropriate to ask, so they just kept rattling around her head with no answer. *How did Nana know Joe? Who was Joe? Where did all these pearls come from? Where were they?*

"Which one this time, Joe? Which one fits this occasion?" Nana asked Joe the question, and Joe's eyes lit up. She'd obviously asked him this same question many times before, but this time the question seemed new to him.

"Wait, Joe picks your pearls?" Teá was astounded!

"You wanted to know how I choose my pearls, and I'm showing you," Nana answered, as if that was a sufficient response for all the questions.

"So, what? You tell Joe what the situation is, what *pearl of wisdom* you want to teach, and he farms just the right pearl for you?" Teá was fascinated by the revelation.

"Pearl of wisdom?" Joe was confused.

Nana's grin spread wide across her face. "Nope, I just ask Joe to pick a pearl."

This did not ease Teá's mind at all. Nana asked a stranger to pick a pearl for Teá, and that was the one used for the pearl of wisdom? But Joe didn't know what a pearl of wisdom was?

The questions were multiplying at this point but everybody else seemed to think they'd been answered.

"I've picked pearls out for your Nana for years. I don't know what she does with them but she must've bought over a hundred pearls from me."

A hundred pearls? The questions just kept coming into Teá's head. Who else gets pearls? Teá had not received a hundred pearls but there must be more of Nana's pearls of wisdom out there somewhere. Teá thought of her sister. She was sure her sister had received as many pearls as Teá. She and Nana were close too, but that was still nowhere near hundreds. Teá wracked her brain, trying to think where hundreds of Nana's pearls may have gone.

"Wait! This isn't even what I meant when I asked how you picked your pearls. And who else gets pearls? Where do these pearls come from?" The questions were tumbling from Teá's mouth faster than she thought them.

"I told you, Joe farms them." As they talked, Joe put on some magnifying glasses. They were huge, and made him look like he had bugs' eyes. He took the glasses off and exclaimed,

"Here it is! This is it, Nana." Nana? Joe called Nana, *Nana*. Had he said that before, and Teá was just too stunned to notice? Did he even know Nana's name? More questions.

Joe rolled the pearl into a familiar velvet bag like the ones Teá had opened countless times before. He tied the drawstrings into a loose knot and handed it over to Nana.

"Thanks Joe! It is so great to see you, but we won't keep you. I know you're busy sorting. We'll see ourselves out. See you soon!" Joe fixed his large glasses back over his eyes, giving him the bug's eye look again, and pored over the pearls that were laid across the towel on the counter.

"See ya. Bye Teá!" Joe sounded distracted by his work already, as Nana and Teá made their way back out the door they came in.

They walked down the long dock, down the stairs to the driveway, which could have been an ocean scene, and silently got into the car.

They put on their seatbelts and Nana roared the Mustang to life. She pushed the button to activate the convertible top and put it securely in the covered position.

"It's a long drive on the interstate from here and I just want to ride in comfort now. Besides, your hair is crazy," Nana said, explaining her reasoning for putting the top back, but still neglecting to explain any of the other things Teá was wondering.

Teá instinctively lowered the sun visor to look into the mirror and gasped at the sight of her wind-blown hair. She laughed, imagining what she and Nana must have looked like together in his beach house. "Nana, you never cease to amaze me," was all Teá could say as Nana started the drive back to the interstate.

"Who? Me? Why?"

Teá laughed out loud, "Oh, you think you have questions. I have questions! This trek did not even answer my original question. What I wanted to know, Nana, is how you choose which of your lessons need a pearl and how you choose your pearls of wisdom, not how you choose your pearls themselves. While it was nothing short of amazing to see how you choose your pearls, I am still curious, how do you choose the pearls of wisdom?"

Nana grinned, "I am answering both. You saw how I choose my pearls, and now *this* will answer how I choose the pearl of wisdom," Nana answered, as she handed the velvet bag she had just gotten from Joe over to her granddaughter.

"Knowing everything you do matters, understanding which relationships deserve priority, healthy boundaries, and forgiveness all are choices. It is important for all of your choices to be made wisely. Some would say to pick your battle. Determine what is, and sometimes what is not worth fighting for. Choosing wisely includes figuring out what is not necessary to address. Some of the best choices we can make in our lives are to *not* act. If what you are fighting over—what you are choosing, is not going to matter five minutes from now; if it is not going to inconvenience you beyond that short five-minute mark, please choose not to pursue it.

A person only has 24 hours in a day, 168 in a week, 8736 in a year. Spending your energy fighting battles that are not yours to fight is a waste of precious time, a waste of the limited hours you have. When you have a choice to respond or to not respond, take your time. Be decisive but understand the impact that your choices—your responses, will have on those around you. If it will not have a lasting impact, let it go.

Just as I let the non-important picking of the pearl be determined by somebody who is not invested in the process, you too, should let the non-important decisions go. However, the important lesson that is behind each pearl is decided very diligently through thought and prayer. In each area of your life, know which are the non-important decisions, and which ones require prayer. Let go of the non-essential, but embrace the ever-so important one.

Pick your battles, Teá. Know which ones are yours to fight, which battles need to be surrendered to the Lord, and which ones are essential."

Ponderings of a Pearl

1. Dinner table fights and stuffed animals seem like silly things for Teá to stress about. It is hard to give up control of things you see as necessary, but not all things are worth fighting over. Are there silly things that you let ruin your day, or invade your thoughts, that you should let go of?

2. Some wars are worth fighting though, and knowing what those are—putting priorities in place, will help you to know what battles are worth fighting for. Are there battles you have in your life that are worth the fight and energy? Could you put more energy into those areas if you let go of the little things?

3. Some battles need to be let go of, others need to be surrendered. Is there a particular battle you're fighting that you have no control over and no way of resolving it? That is the battle that needs to be surrendered to the Lord. Pray to Him and surrender it to Him.

4. 1 Peter 5:7-11 gives a perfect example of what we, as believers, are to do with our worries, our concerns, and our battles. They are to be cast upon the one who can handle them. He will lift you up and make you strong enough to fight, if that is what you are supposed to do. What battles in your life need to be cast upon your Savior?

··· 6 ···

Finding Hope

"God did this so that, by two unchangeable things in which it is impossible for God to lie, we who have fled to take hold of the hope set before us may be greatly encouraged. We have this hope as an anchor for the soul, firm and secure. It enters the inner sanctuary behind the curtain."

~Heb. 6:18-19

THE DRIVE TO the freeway from Joe's beach house seemed quicker than the drive to his home, probably because of the light mood in the car and the new found pearl that Teá now possessed. She was thinking about the times she could've remained so much more peaceful, had she just picked her battles. She and Owen definitely needed to discuss the food issues at the dinner table, but she didn't need to hold so fiercely to her opinions. She was sorry that all Harley's stuffed animals were already gone. How silly, what she had been willing to cause such strife over.

Once back on the interstate, the conversation started again between Teá and Nana. "Thanks, as always, for the pearl, Nana," Teá stated.

"Of course. I really feel like you've come a long way in the past year and this one brings some wisdom to get you through hard times that will arise in your life," Nana said, wise as ever.

Teá smiled at Nana's remark. It was funny how some pearls had to be revisited, relearned, over and over, while others served their purpose from the start. The pearl remained in the collection, but the lesson it taught was over. Her forgiveness pearl, for example, was one that she often had to reflect on, which was why she was so thankful Owen thought to make it into something she could wear continually.

"Can you tell me where we are going now?" Teá asked hopefully.

"Nope," Nana said, without missing a beat.

The car was heading down the same road Teá was on a year ago when Harley made her so mad. Teá was confident that whatever Nana had planned was in the same city the conference had been in.

• • •

Teá again started reflecting over the previous year's events. She remembered how she felt in that van after the conference.

She'd felt so lonely—a car full of women, but no friends. A church full of people, but no hope for any connections. A house full of family, but no real relationships with any of them. No wonder she was angry all the time. Every little thing had seemed to set her off.

Working through the grudges she continued to hold, choosing to forgive those that had wronged her, choosing to reconcile relationships that needed it, and letting go of the ones that didn't, Teá started to relate more to the women in that car. She began opening herself up more to the church family that adored her, and she was able to make her house a home full of strong family relationships.

The boundaries she and Owen had put up in order to keep the peace in their home prevented more issues that could cause hurt. Intentionally setting boundaries and enforcing them made their marriage stronger. Funny, the things she never imagined would bother her easy-going husband were things he insisted needed boundaries. For example, one time he had asked her not to get a ride home from a male coworker. Her car wouldn't start, and she wanted to just get home. She knew Owen could stop and look at it on his way home, so she was comfortable getting a ride from the owner of the restaurant. Owen texted back, "I have to put a boundary there. Please don't be alone with another man." This, and all the other boundaries, helped to solidify what their marriage meant.

This is why Nana's next pearl, given to Owen, was so important, so vital. Owen needed a reminder that they were in this together and that he had to put his priorities straight in order for the marriage to succeed. Shortly after receiving that pearl, Teá and Owen decided to make new vows to each other—a new covenant. Owen told Teá that he believed the purpose of their marriage was to show their kids what a marriage relationship was supposed to look like. He acknowledged that by putting their marriage ahead of everything but

Jesus, he was giving their marriage the place in their priorities it deserved.

Teá could feel the tears start to form as she recalled the previous year's events. The next pearl brought to mind her friend, Shannon. Teá had encouraged Shannon to start attending church and to seek counseling for herself and her husband. Shannon had told her just the other day, "I didn't think there was any hope for our marriage. I was convinced it was over, but we are happier now than ever before, and it happened so quickly." Shannon was much more pleasant during their afternoon visits, and they had even started reading a devotional book together. Teá wondered what Shannon and her husband did to make that happen and was quickly reminded that it was the decisions Teá made that allowed it to happen. Every decision she ever made, or would make again, could impact many people. What an awesome reminder too, that Shannon and her husband sticking together through their struggles would have a huge impact on their children, extended family, and even their friends, like Teá.

Which brought her and Nana to here and now, a full year later, driving into the same city that had started the year's events. Teá was a different person. She remembered the feelings she felt that day: discouragement, failure, sadness, and frustration, but they were a distant memory. She remembered what she saw and heard that day with Harley and the fight that ensued with Owen over his eldest daughter's antics. She remembered them as though she were a different person. Teá had changed so much in this short year, she no longer held grudges. She always tried to find peace where she could and she was confident her marriage would survive, because now she knew that she was fighting for not only her happiness, but for the legacy she and Owen would leave their children.

"Nana, are we stopping here?" Teá wondered if their road trip was about over, or if Nana was going to continue.

"No, just a few more minutes," Nana answered, as she signaled to get off the interstate.

This is the same exit to the convention center we took last year, Teá thought to herself. The Chick-fil-A was right up the street, where Harley had made such a scene.

It suddenly occurred to Teá what Nana had done. They were travelling back to the same conference.

"Nana, are we going to the women's conference?" Teá asked, giddy with excitement. She remembered hearing about it advertised at church, but the women decided not to make the trek this year, so she hadn't thought any more of it.

"I thought it'd be fun." Nana said with a grin.

"We are super early, Nana. Last year it didn't start until Friday evening. Why are we here so early? What are your plans?"

"I thought it'd be fun to spend two full days in the city. I wanted to get an early start this morning, to get to the conference by noon," Nana answered.

"Ok, but there really is nothing to do in this area. They probably don't even open the doors for a few more hours." Teá didn't understand why Nana wanted to get to the conference a full six hours before it started. If she remembered right, worship started at 6:00 p.m. last year, and it was almost noon.

Nana pulled into the convention center parking lot without answering Teá. It felt weird to be parking in such a big empty lot, but Nana backed the convertible into a spot close to the front entrance, turned off the ignition, gathered her purse and a bag Teá hadn't noticed, containing Nana's sacred Bible.

"Do you want me to carry anything?" Teá asked, as she prepared to exit the car.

"Nope, I got it," Nana answered.

"I still don't know why we are so early, Nana. The conference doesn't start for a long time."

"Why do you worry so much?" Nana asked Teá. "Do you think I don't have enough wits about me to tell time, to manage my own plan—something fun for me and my grand-daughter?" Nana wasn't offended or irritated. Her rhetorical questions were delivered jokingly.

"Nana, you seriously never cease to amaze me," Teá answered, in response to her grandmother's strange and quirky ways.

They entered the empty convention center through the front doors. Nobody was there yet to collect tickets or to stop them. Nana navigated her way around the main entrance of the auditorium, Teá staying in step with her Nana, letting her lead the way. Teá gave up on asking questions; Nana wasn't answering them anyway. It was probably a quarter of a mile walk around the outside of the huge arena. Workers were busy getting concession stands prepared and there were tables set up with boxes of books waiting to be unpacked and sold. There were a few people wandering around preparing for the big event that evening and nobody seemed to notice them, probably because Nana knew exactly where she was going.

Teá began to notice a theme on the merchandise tables. She saw a few banners hung by the production crew and thought it strange that one word printed and displayed everywhere was *hope*. She tried to remember the decorations, tables, and themes from the year previous, but her Nana was right. Before the forgiveness pearl was delivered, she had lost everything she learned at last year's conference due to her unforgiving heart, including the theme.

Finally, Nana and Teá came across some doors on one side of the auditorium that were labeled "Staging Area," and "Dressing Rooms." Nana barged into the door that was set up as a staging area like she belonged there, like she owned the place. Teá tried to stop her. "Nana, we can't just go in there!" But Nana ignored her and went inside.

There was a huge conference table in the middle of the room, surrounded by windows that looked out into what Teá assumed was the backside of the convention center. All she could see was a cement parking garage and traffic. Inside the room, the conference table was strewn with what looked like take-out containers, miscellaneous papers, pens, and an assortment of things used for a meeting. There was a dozen or more people wandering aimlessly around the room. One person was seated on a small love seat in the corner of the room and another was sitting with legs crossed on the floor in the middle of the large space. Mostly everybody else was walking slowly as they prayed. It took a minute for Teá to realize they were praying and when she did, she immediately felt like an even bigger intruder. Nana had just barged into a prayer room.

Teá bowed her head reverently and tried to grab Nana's sleeve to pull her out of the room, but as she reached out to grab Nana, she noticed she was no longer in front of her. Nana had made her way toward the conference table, joining in the prayers. She had her arms raised, and she was mouthing a silent supplication. Teá didn't know what to do. She didn't understand how Nana knew where to come, what to do or what to pray, so she made her way to an empty corner of the room and watched.

Teá watched these people pour out their hearts to God. Some prayed aloud for the conference, for the hearts that would be changed, for the words from God that would bring people closer to Him. They prayed for each-others' families as they travelled with the conference and they prayed for one another. Mostly, though, their prayers were silent and personal. Teá felt like an intruder, invading such a private moment for these strangers. She was studying each one but they seemed oblivious to her intrusion. She wondered why they were there; they clearly were not just there like she was, clueless as to their purpose. Were they the worship band? The speaker's staff?

Teá didn't know, until she looked closely at the lady sitting on the love seat in the corner opposite from which Teá was trying to hide. She immediately recognized her as the speaker at last year's conference. Nana had just dragged Teá into the speaker's private prayer meeting. Teá flushed with embarrassment at such an intrusion. What was Nana thinking? You can't just barge into the room of a woman of that caliber, and you can't just interrupt such a woman's prayers. Teá started to get more uneasy when, as if on cue, the woman stood up from the love seat, and began to pray out loud.

"Father, God, help me to spread this message you have placed in my heart in such a way that the thousands of women coming tonight will understand in a personal, convicting way. Help me to reiterate Your message of hope so that everybody in attendance tonight will leave refreshed, restored, and recharged. You tell us that Your word will not return void but will accomplish what pleases you. Let that be the case here tonight. It is always in Jesus' beautiful name we pray, amen." Everyone joined her with the final word, and they all scattered, ready to go forth and do what they had come there to accomplish.

Teá could feel a heavy presence in the room, like an electrical charge that was ready to ignite—something she had never experience before. She wondered to herself, *is that what prayer is supposed to do?* She had never felt that before.

Almost immediately, it seemed, Teá was alone in the room with Nana and the speaker from the conference.

"Nana!"

"Megan!" that was the speaker's name, it occurred to Teá as soon as she embraced her grandmother with the same familiarity that Nana had with seemingly everybody on this planet. "Thank you so much for coming and praying with us. It means the world to me." Megan exclaimed when she pulled her Nana away from her hug, holding her at arm's length and looked lovingly in Nana's eyes.

"Sorry I was a little late; we had to make a pit stop along the way," Nana said sheepishly.

"I told you not to hurry; if you could make it, great. If not…no big deal." Megan answered Nana with a smile, then turned to look at Teá, who was doing her best to try to blend in with the wall.

"You must be Teá. I've heard so much about you recently. How are you? Any offspring of Nana's has the biggest blessing in their life," Megan said to Teá, with a huge grin.

"I, umm . . . uh, yeah, she's pretty great," Teá stammered. She was a little star-struck, taken aback that this woman knew her Nana, and entirely shocked by the gravity of the situation.

"Pretty great? She's my absolute favorite!" Megan said with a smile that led all the way up through her eyes. "Everyone else has already eaten, but I waited for you. Please won't you two join me for lunch?" She turned around toward the conference room with the to-go containers. "I ordered-in Chinese; I hope that's okay with you both."

"I love Chinese. I've been looking forward to this for so long," Nana said as she started making her way to the table.

Teá pealed herself out of the corner she had been standing in and made her way to the table to join Nana and Megan.

So strange, she thought, I was at her conference last year and wasted the time spent with my own anger. Now here I am sitting in front of her . . . about to enjoy lunch with her. How did she know Nana?

Teá was too star-struck, too speechless, to join in the conversation unfolding in front of her. Nana shared with this amazing woman of God some of the struggles she'd had in her own life. She shared the idea of "pearls of wisdom" for those she loved, and that she often sent pearls based on things she wished somebody had told her, in pivotal moments of her own life.

Teá was listening intently because she had wondered so often how and why Nana had started the tradition of sending pearls. She'd wondered where the idea came from, even asking in the car ride to the pearl farm, but she'd been too overwhelmed with Joe's beach house to follow through with asking the question. Teá learned more about her beloved Nana by watching her interact with this other woman of God, it was almost like Nana was speaking with her the same way she spoke with Teá.

Nana then started asking her own questions. "When did you begin speaking; when was that desire put into your heart?" Nana asked.

"My story is similar to yours. Like you, I teach the things I wish someone would have taught me in pivotal moments. I look back in the valleys of my own life and wonder what I missed because I didn't know better. That is what I want to teach every time I deliver a message—I want to reach into somebody's hopelessness and give them the hope that I so desperately needed. I haven't always been a student of the Word, and I haven't always been a believer in Jesus Christ."

There's that word again, Teá thought. She had felt hopelessness too? No way had this woman who seemed to have all the wisdom of the world, all the wisdom of the Word, ever felt hopeless as well.

"I was without hope for a very long time, which is how this particular conference theme finally came into my heart. I had been wanting to explain hope, but I struggled with it so much that I didn't know where to begin." She smiled, recollecting something. "You have to begin right there, don't you? Right in the middle of hope. I finally began in the Word of God and the rest unfolded right in front of me."

Nana reached over and squeezed Teá's hand. She must've noticed Teá perk up and start to pay closer attention.

"What is hope? Is it a feeling, an emotion, or a wish?" Teá couldn't maintain her silence anymore; all this talk about hope had her curious. Finally, she felt somebody could answer her questions. "I am so tired of hearing people say, 'I hope that happens,' or 'I hope that doesn't happen again,' or 'that situation is hopeless.'" Teá started to get emotional in her plea to this stranger. "I hate hope. I hate all the emptiness behind it. I hate that everybody says they have hope, but they don't seem to know what it means. I hate that people always tell me you have to have hope, but nobody can give it to me, or offer it as something that I can possess." Teá was almost in tears. She was embarrassed to be this emotional in front of such an influential person, but she had had enough, and the feelings were overtaking her in a way that she could not really stop or control.

With a smile, and no ill-will intended, Megan answered Teá, "Please wait until you hear me tonight. Please let's pray that God will finally give you something worth hoping for with my message." She reached over and grasped Teá's hand and prayed a petition that filled Teá with so much emotion, so much power, that she was overcome with tears.

After the prayer, Megan excused herself to get ready for the evening in her dressing room, but she invited Teá and Nana to stay as long as they wanted. She also told them to go look at the different books and merchandise available. She handed them both tickets, and told Teá, "I'll be looking for you."

Teá and Nana spent the rest of the afternoon exploring the huge conference center. They stopped to look at the vendors' offerings, and Teá grabbed a few trinkets for the kids: necklaces for each of the girls and a cool bracelet for Lincoln. She thumbed through a few couples' devotionals to see if there was anything of interest to her in her relationship with Owen, and she and Nana were both surprised to find a gorgeous pearl bracelet for sale. Neither of them were interested in purchasing it because, even though it was beautiful, there was no meaning behind these pearls.

While it was fun to spend the afternoon with Nana, Teá still had many questions. "How did Nana know this speaker? What were these emotions Teá couldn't shake after praying with her? How precious was tonight going to be?" She was almost giddy with excitement for the conference to start, but she was curious about Megan. How did she know what to pray for? Had Nana shared with this stranger what Teá was struggling with? It took Teá's breath away at the thought, the embarrassment; she tried so hard to keep her secrets . . . secret. She felt like a failure when she looked over her past. Surely Nana wouldn't have divulged these things to a stranger.

When Nana noticed the crowds entering the conference center, she suggested to Teá that they go find their seats. They looked over their tickets to see which entry to use in order to access their seat. The huge, round arena had several different levels, with separate entrances to each level, so they had to navigate and wind their way to their row. Teá and Nana were seated directly in front of the stage. There was room between their seats and the stage for crews to work, and their area was raised off the ground in order to be level with the stage.

Teá remembered from the year previous that she and the women from church had been up three stories of stairs and several configurations of escalators. They could barely make out the worship team or the speaker on the stage, and had focused mainly on the jumbo-trons that were elevated high above them.

Teá marveled at how Nana was able to score such great seats and personal access to this popular, well known speaker. Yet here they were, and the worship was beginning.

Teá always wanted to worship the way she saw others do. She wanted to feel the movement of the Lord the way others claimed, but she always felt like she was faking it during the worship services she attended at church, or in other scenarios like this. Nana, for example, was a joy to watch as she worshiped. She had no problem raising her hands or shouting with joy at a particularly touching moment. Nana danced and swayed with the music and clapped along as the conference opened with a worship set. Teá stood, unable to sit, and bowed her head when it felt appropriate, but typically she was stoic during worship. She often wondered if there was something wrong with her. Did she even know how to worship?

The band was incredible! Teá enjoyed watching them from this close, and she loved worshiping next to her Nana. During the final song Nana grabbed Teá's hand and Teá could feel an electricity between them, similar to what she felt when Megan had prayed for her just hours earlier. She couldn't help but raise her other hand to the sky, her face turned upward, and instantly thoughts of peace and thankfulness filled her head, but even more so, her heart. She didn't want the song to end. Her eyes were closed and the piano was still playing. She could hear voices throughout the auditorium praying and there were more prayers coming from the speaker. Eventually, Teá heard Megan's familiar voice praying about the conference and the words she was about to speak.

Teá finally opened her eyes and released Nana's hand. Megan looked larger than when she saw her earlier—grand, and with a commanding presence on stage. She had on more make-up and her hair was set differently than the informal look she had earlier, when Teá and Nana ate lunch with her. She was wearing black pants, a black shirt, and a gorgeous bright red jacket, with shoes to match. Everything about her on stage seemed to contradict Teá's experience as she met with her earlier that day. During the lunch and prayer time, she had worn jeans and a shirt. Her hair had been clean but not styled, and Teá didn't remember her wearing much make-up. She vaguely remembered something she'd heard about having to wear a lot of make up on stage in order to not appear washed out under the bright lights and cameras that were everywhere.

As soon as Megan opened her mouth Teá felt the same familiar comfort she had experienced earlier. It was almost as if they were back in the conference room enjoying a private lunch together. Megan had a podium in front of her and a stool off to the side, but she wasn't behind the podium and was standing far away from the stool when she began with words that made Teá's heart jump into her throat.

"Hope, deferred, makes the heart sick."

Teá was flabbergasted! Teá remembered all the hope messages Nana had given her over the last year. She remembered telling Nana how much she hated hope, she was tired of hope, and she didn't understand hope. The speaker continued, "Proverbs tells us that. What does it mean, though? What does deferred hope look like, and what even *is* hope?

"My husband is a huge Nebraska football fan." The entire auditorium went up in a roar as the speaker admitted this. Teá looked over at Nana, who smiled widely. *Is that how Nana knew this speaker?* Teá wondered.

"I am not. I am not from Nebraska, and I know nothing about the team nor, really, the sport." The speaker continued with a smile, once the roar from the crowd died down. "My husband can quote the stats, knows how many national championships the team has won, and can tell you which coaches and players earned them. He knows a lot about Nebraska football. He often dresses in red and he very rarely does not have an "N" somewhere in his clothing. One time early in our marriage, we were walking through an airport. He was dressed in red garb, from head to toe. We were walking quickly, trying to catch a connecting flight from somewhere across the terminal, when somebody yelled loudly, 'Gooooo Biiiiig Reeeeed'." My usually quiet, mild-mannered husband shocked me. I mean, he literally made me jump out of my boots when he screamed back at this stranger, 'Go Big Red!' I had no idea what had just happened and both men acted like it was a perfectly normal exchange."

Teá laughed and cheered along with the crowd. This was perfectly normal banter for Nebraska fans and Nana probably yelled louder than anybody else.

"It made me wonder," the speaker continued, "how much hope was deferred to that team. How much hope did my husband, that stranger, and all the fans for Nebraska football defer to that team, to that coach, to the next big playmaker that was recruited? You see, because hope deferred makes the heart sick."

The stadium quieted quickly at this harsh realization brought to them by the speaker, but she continued.

"How much hope, I wonder, is deferred to marriage? How much hope is deferred to a spouse? How much hope is deferred to the economy, to a job, to the stock market for that matter? How often do we, as fallen, sinful humans, defer our hope to something that is not able to anchor our soul?"

"The Strong's Dictionary gives a lot of definitions for the word defer: to draw, sound, prolong, develop, march, remove, delay. The two synonyms that make me pause are: to forbear, and to give. How many people have given hope, or deferred hope, to the wrong things?

"The author of Hebrews called hope 'an anchor to our soul.' Surely, the kind of hope that we put into a team, or even into some of our most valued possessions or relationships cannot anchor our soul. An anchor is used to stabilize a ship. It is a vital instrument upon every sea-going vessel. The anchor keeps the ship solidly in position. It does not allow the ship to sway so much that damage will be caused, and an anchor does not allow a ship to drift at all. When we put our hope in a sports team, there is not much strength in that anchor. When we put our hope in a job, or in our finances, our anchor is only as strong as the number of zero's in our checking account. If we put our hope in our marriage, in our relationships, the ship will sway and drift when the first fight happens, when things get really difficult."

Teá had tears streaming down her face at this revelation. She remembered all the times she had put her hope in these things. She had hoped Owen would be the one to save her, that this marriage would make her happy, to leave a legacy for her family. She believed that the stability in Owen's job should have been enough to avoid the financial conflicts they experienced. She had deferred all of her hope, she thought, as the speaker continued.

"When we put our hope in the solid rock that is Jesus Christ, that anchor digs in, firm and secure. That anchor, in fact, holds so tight that even the troubles in our marriage, even the crash of the stock market, or the sudden loss of employment cannot cause the ship to drift, or even sway.

What is even more beautiful is that when our hope is not deferred, and is given solidly to the play maker, the ultimate creator, the only Savior of our soul; when we hope in nothing less than Jesus, he comes into our marriage and blesses that union more than we could ever ask, think or imagine. He comes into our finances and makes them align to His will in ways that we never believed possible. He gives us favor in our job and most importantly, He gives us freedom from having to worry if that anchor will hold. Scripture tells us, "…hope does not disappoint, because the love of God has been poured out within our hearts through the Holy Spirit who was given to us."

As Megan made her point, and she grew louder and louder, the crowd matched her energy and clapped or raised their hands in the victories she was declaring from the stage.

Teá was quiet, though. She sat down in her seat next to her Nana and sobbed. Her tears were simply a representation of everything she had been feeling. She felt broken, her heart sick, because she had deferred her hope.

Teá realized during the conference that she *had* given her heart to Jesus. She was saved and there was no doubt she would go to Heaven should she die, but she had not surrendered everything to Him like she was instructed, like Nana had tried so long to help her do.

She wanted Owen to provide many things that only Jesus could. She had wanted this life, this world to give her the things that would bring peace and satisfaction to her soul, but she refused to acknowledge that without Christ, without the Holy Spirit bringing these things, she would always remain hopeless; she would always hate hope.

The worship closing the conference felt different to Teá. She felt a stirring, a longing for more. She didn't want the conference to end, because she felt if she left this place, she would be going back to the same defeat she had experienced all along. Teá didn't want to leave the atmosphere she had come to know and love.

As Megan prepared to pray for the final time that night, she made another statement as if she was reading Teá's mind. She said, "You might be dreading going home, wondering what is next, how more to expand this journey toward hope, but I have one more parting thought about Nebraska football to leave you with.

Even though, when Memorial Stadium is full of raging fans, it becomes the 3rd most populated city in the State of Nebraska, and the tension and atmosphere is incredible, even though the cheering of those fans can be deafening at times, the excitement of the stadium gives the home team a significant advantage over their opponent, and even though the game lasts for sometimes over four hours, the team spirit and pride does not continue when they are not playing.

When the victory goes to the Nebraska team, when the stadium is empty, when the seats are vacant and when all those fans full of hope for their team are driving home, the spirit that was felt in that stadium is gone.

But rest assured, the Spirit living inside of you tonight will still be with you when you are driving home. He will be with you in your conversations about this event because Christ, the one you decided to put your full hope into, will never leave you or forsake you."

Again, Teá was crying as the speaker blessed them with another prayer, before bringing the conference to a conclusion.

Ponderings of a Pearl

1. While Teá didn't receive a pearl during the conference, she did have a lot to consider, who, or what was she putting her hope in? Who, or what, are you putting your hope in?

2. If hope deferred makes your heart sick, can you find areas where your heart is sick because you are putting hope in something that is not strong enough to anchor your soul?

3. Read Hebrews 6:19, and pray that God remind you of the hope, a steadfast hope, that was secured behind the veil.

CPSIA information can be obtained
at www.ICGtesting.com
Printed in the USA
BVHW041345041120
592505BV00012B/573

9 781647 464714